West Country
Edited by Steve Twelvetree

First published in Great Britain in 2004 by:
Young Writers
Remus House
Coltsfoot Drive
Peterborough
PE2 9JX
Telephone: 01733 890066
Website: www.youngwriters.co.uk

All Rights Reserved

© Copyright Contributors 2004

SB ISBN 1 84460 441 1

Foreword

Young Writers was established in 1991 and has been passionately devoted to the promotion of reading and writing in children and young adults ever since. The quest continues today. Young Writers remains as committed to engendering the fostering of burgeoning poetic and literary talent as ever.

This year's Young Writers competition has proven as vibrant and dynamic as ever and we are delighted to present a showcase of the best poetry from across the UK. Each poem has been carefully selected from a wealth of *Once Upon A Rhyme* entries before ultimately being published in this, our twelfth primary school poetry series.

Once again, we have been supremely impressed by the overall high quality of the entries we have received. The imagination, energy and creativity which has gone into each young writer's entry made choosing the best poems a challenging and often difficult but ultimately hugely rewarding task - the general high standard of the work submitted amply vindicating this opportunity to bring their poetry to a larger appreciative audience.

We sincerely hope you are pleased with our final selection and that you will enjoy *Once Upon A Rhyme West Country* for many years to come.

Contents

Donna Janes (14)	1
Daniel Jones (7)	1

Ashley Down Junior School
Floren Scrafton (10)	2
Lateefah Ngozi (10)	3
Billie Skuse-Denley (9)	3
Fionn McMahon-Parkes (10)	4
Lawrence Hewlett-Walker (10)	4
Jasmine Manson (11)	5
Mattias Tamar-Gill (9)	5
Lauren Russ-Constant (10)	6
Elle Douel (10)	6
Chris Maddix (10)	7
Ana Ryan Flinn (9)	8
Lorna Besley (8)	8

Colston's Girls' School
Christine Howie (10)	9
Claudia Lowe (10)	9
Kathryn Parker (10)	10
Sophia Malik (10)	10
Laura Sinclair (10)	11
Alannah Black (11)	11
Rachel Quaife (10)	12
Paris Olivia May Vassell (11)	12
Antonia Self (10)	13
Corinne Walker (10)	13
Josie Pearson (11)	14
Frances Nelson (10)	14
Charlotte Head (10)	15
Georgiana Ward (10)	15
Isabella Baldo (11)	15
Emily Hurse (10)	16
Ebony Jarrett (10)	16
Kate Glynn (10)	17
Shelley Silvester (11)	17
Beth Norman (11)	18

Yasmin Kingdon (10)   18
Chantelle Sims (11)   19

Colston's Lower School
Amy Spreadbury (10)   19
Andrew Fowles (10)   20
Emma Fredericks (10)   20
Benjamin Moore (9)   21
C J Adams (10)   21
Jacob Nowak (9)   22
Alex Denton (7)   22
Kayleigh Pincott (9)   23
Ellie Diamond (9)   23
Jack Willson-Patel (9)   24
Jon Roper (9)   24
Samuel Miller (9)   25
Harrison Ball (7)   25
Isabelle Webb (7)   26
Harry Ford (8)   27
Georgina Morrison (9)   28
Isabella Yaxley (8)   28
Greg Herbert (10)   29
Georgia Masters (9)   29
Danielle Anderson (9)   30
Ben Woodward (9)   30
Emma Poole (9)   31
Alex Wakley (9)   31
Olivia Powell (10)   32
Claire Aldridge (9)   32
Kerala Drew (10)   33
Adam Rivers (9)   33
Jay O'Forrester (11)   34
Robert Eden (10)   35
Christopher Lynden (11)   36
Nathan Patten (9)   36
Dan White (11)   37
Oreofe Majekodunmi (7)   38
Ian Clark (11)   39
William Philip (11)   40
Alex Yuill (9)   40
Ben Sullivan (9)   41

Jonathan Lowrie (10)	41
Max Allen (9)	42
Letisha Gollop (10)	42
Constantinos Polyviou (10)	43
Jack Collins (10)	43
Max Tarr (10)	44
Oliver Philip	44
Lottie Davies (11)	45
Charlotte Hope (10)	45
Oliver Denton (8)	46
Raymond Hodges (10)	46
Luke Bailey (11)	47
Aaron Sealey-Grant (11)	47
Arun Mali (11)	48
Robert Callaway (8)	48
Sam Crew (10)	49
David Attwood (8)	49
Ellie Carder (8)	50
Rhiannon Adams (9)	50
Jay Chauhan (8)	51
Jack Digby (8)	51
Sara Procter (9)	52
James Baber (9)	52
Folu Majek (9)	53
Ronnie Arathoon (8)	53
Steven Hanney (11)	54
Alice Harding (8)	55
Ben Helps (8)	55
Alex Knight (8)	56
Maria Jones (8)	56
Lillie-Mae Maddox (8)	57
Anna Thomas (7)	57
Eva Polyviou (8)	58
Joshua Wanklyn (7)	58
Sandeep Vijay (7)	59

Coniston Primary School

Alice Fillingham (9)	59
Jack Trueman (9)	59
Leah Tozer (9)	60
Zoe Broomfield (10)	60

Leanne Couchman (10)	60
Stacey Peard (8)	61
Danielle Lock (9)	61
Luke Winchcombe (10)	61
Callan Bourne (9)	62
Jack Skinner (9)	62
Toni Lawrence (10)	62
Alya Strode (8)	63
Daniel Rees (8)	63
Lana Skuse (8)	63
Zoë Parry (7)	64
Chelsea Thomas (11)	64
Daniella Prowse (10)	64
Stacey Coleman (11)	65
Joe Shipley (11)	65
Lisa Coghlan (10)	65
Daniel Harvey (11)	66
Sacha Ware (11)	66

Fair Furlong Primary School

Jordan Blammon (10)	66
Lee Spray (10)	67
Conor Malin (9)	67
James Wall (9)	68
Kieran Giddings (9)	68
Leon Dew (9)	69
Paige Batchelor (9)	69
Tracy Thomas (10)	70
Amie Purnell (10)	70
Heather Milton (9)	71
Khadija Ali Hassan (9)	71
Kieran Westgate (9)	72
Curtis Rush (11)	72
Jack Tucker (10)	73
Chantell Searle (10)	73
Hayley Delaney (10)	74
George Gray (10)	74
James Langridge (10)	75
Nick Lathrope (10)	75
Ben Yearsley (10)	76
Kirsty Lester (9)	76

Toni Hazell (10)   77
Katie Andow (10)   77
Paige Nelmes (9)   78
Shonnie Coles (9)   78
Sarah Lane (9)   79

Hillcrest Primary School
Albie Mayo-Hagues (8)   79
Anna Jordan (9)   80
Safa Iqbal (8)   80
Stan Portus (10)   81
Lauren Aquilina (8)   81
Melissa Almeida (8)   82
Karis Godbeer (9)   82
Rosy Pearson (10)   83
Elise McDonald (9)   83
Tom Netto (10)   84
Alex Sinclair (11)   84
Joanna Hay (10)   85
Billy Golding (10)   85
Chelsea Walton (10)   86
James Sharman (10)   86
Harry Cox   87
Sheldon Golding (10)   87
Natasha Morris (10)   88
Eva Freeman (11)   88
Helena Ferguson (10)   89
Jessie Greenwood (9)   89
Ben Jester (11)   90
Emma Cresswell (10)   90
Ellie Pope (11)   91
Aisha Sahi (10)   91
Ede Dugdale-Close (8)   92
Lily Bland (11)   92
Holly Baker (11)   93
Harry Atkins (7)   93
Oscar Pope (8)   94
Tegen George (8)   94
Anna Fleming (8)   95
Dexter Doling-Baker (8)   95
Tomek Pieczora (7)   96

Cai Burton (7)	96
Jemima Harrison (7)	96
Lois Cox (8)	97
Kira Rich (8)	97
Alice Wilson McNeal (10)	98
Clare Thompson (7)	98
Madeline Finch (8)	99
Polly Rorison (7)	99
Sophie Rippington (9)	100
Florrie Badley (8)	100
Frankie Pigott-Plowden (9)	101
Nikolei Joseph Suray (7)	101
Jack Boxall (10)	102
Ali-Ahmed Malik (9)	102
Ella Maggs (9)	103
Laura Ferguson (9)	103
Finny Nugent (9)	104
Imogen Hawkins (8)	104
Ben Mason (8)	105
Syeda Zahra (8)	105
Matilda Everett (10)	106
Hannah Wyatt (8)	106
Michael Sinclair (9)	107
Jacob Youngs (8)	107
Chris Whitty (8)	107
Ellen Sorohan (10)	108
Edward Davis (9)	108
Gary Bell (10)	109
Patrick Carver (10)	109
Ivo Perry (9)	110
Tara Anderson (8)	110
Samuel Gaunt (9)	111
Sam Gurney (9)	111
Jake Edmonds (9)	112
Oliver Clarke (10)	112
Haroon Ali (10)	113
Jo Nugent (9)	113
Amy Bolton (10)	113
James Cockle (9)	114
Conney Wells (10)	114
Ellen Davies (9)	115
Raeanne Manning (9)	115

Amy Stevenson (8)	116
Jessica Bailey (10)	116
Sean Byrne (10)	117
Sharratt Long (9)	117
Nuha Najihah	117
Liam Barter (9)	118
Alec Coombes (9)	118
Nur Nabilah Zainudin (10)	118
Louisha Stanbridge (9)	119
Bethany Sordnan (10)	119
Oliver Trace (9)	120
Edward Ashby-Hayter (10)	120
Archie Gunning (10)	121
Elspeth Bond (10)	121
Amy Baker (8)	122
Bradley Lewis (9)	122
Alexander Palmer (8)	123
Reuben Leveson-Gower (10)	124

High Down Junior School

Lillie Grimshaw (9)	124
Dillon Eastoe (9)	124

Hotwells Primary School

Joshua Walker (8)	125
Cameron Byrne (8)	125
Maeve Scally (8)	126
Hattie Swingler (8)	126
Evie Miles (8)	127
Jo Thompson (8)	127
Annys Whyatt (9)	127
Hannah Marke-Crooke (9)	128
Ailish Shallcross (8)	128
Keir Byatt (8)	129
Harry Lloyd-Evans (8)	129
Chirag Trivedi (8)	130
Isaac Willis (8)	130
Fred Baker Turner (8)	131
Fleur Baughen (9)	131
Bill Dunn (8)	132
Ngaio Danvers (9)	132

Zoe Sherrell (9)	133
Bala Piti (9)	133
Joe Lanham (8)	133

North Road School
Molly Jenkins (9)	134
Rebecca Lock (9)	134
Zoe Potts (9)	134
Sophie Bolton (9)	135
Beth Staley (9)	135

Overndale School
Charlotte Causon (11)	136
Benjamin Lynskey (7)	136
Francesca Causon (9)	137
Katie Bennett (7)	137
Kerry-Dee Shaw (8)	138
Jack Harris (7)	138
Georgina Daniell (10)	139
Maddie Hopkinson-Buss (7)	139
Megan Mulhall (9)	140
Alexander Harvey (11)	140
Emma Ridley (10)	141
Rosie Pearson (11)	141
Declan Mulhall (11)	142

Rodford Primary School
Sam Davies (10)	142
Alice Phillips (10)	143
Lydia Lambert (10)	144

St Barnabas CE Primary School, Portishead
Sian Pennant-Jones (8)	144
Joanna Cox (9)	145
Olivia Kincaid (10)	145
Rory Atherton (10)	145
Samuel James (10)	146
Simon Shepherd (10)	146
Jess Smith (10)	146

Jack Rekesius (11) & William Ash (10)   147
Jenni Harding (10)   147

St John's CE Primary School, Clifton
Ameena Jassim (8)   147
Clare Hunter Funnell (8)   148
Adam Ebdy (8)   148
Kate Brennan (9)   149
Thea Rogers (8)   149
Evleen Price (8)   150
Josie Brown (9)   150
Jack Whitby (9)   151
Tessa Mathieson (8)   151
Jake Thompson (9)   152
Kaela Jones (9)   152
Emily Perry (8)   153
Danielle Lambert (8)   153

St Mary's CE Primary School, Yate
Joe York (10)   153
Hannen Ashlee (10)   154
Blake Skuse (10)   154
Abigail Woods (11)   155
George Slade (10)   155
Charlotte Northam (9)   156
Katie Pittaway (9)   156
Robert McLeod (11)   157
Jack Smoothy (10)   157
Ashley White (11)   158
Luke Sparrow (10)   158
Bethany Rowsell (10)   159
Jessica Harrod (10)   159
Daniella Spring (9)   160
Emily Davies (10)   160
Alice Dudbridge (10)   161
Hannah Fry (10)   161
Kerry Williams (9)   161
Katie Cardall (9)   162
Laura-Jo Stubbings (10)   162
Sadie Stenner (9)   163
Katie Rogers (9)   163

Olivia Flynn (9)	163
Alex Millichamp (9)	164
Conner Foley (9)	164
Sam Martin (9)	164
Jessica Rudge (9)	165
Ellie Phillips (9)	165
Alice Rogers (9)	165
Lauren Wiltshire (11)	166
Jodie Williams (9)	166
Alex Martin (9)	167
Carl Childs (9)	167
Jack Townsend (9)	167
Jamie Dadd (11)	168
Misha Wiley (10)	168
Philippa Cutts (11)	169
Alaina Herbert (9)	169
Joe McKivitt (10)	170
Cameron Kelly (10)	170
Katie Howell (10)	171
James Faulkner (11)	171
Lewis White (10)	172
Jason Bradford (10)	172
Alex Davies (11)	173
Jake Parsons (9)	173
Adam Fox (10)	174
Bethan Ashlee (9)	174
Nathan Langley (10)	175
Josh Gouge (11)	175
Harley Thorne (10)	176
Sasha Tallis (10)	176
Katherine Powell (10)	177

The Ridge Junior School
Robert Bryden (10)	177
Hannah Dicks (11)	178
Katie Wilkinson (11)	178
Emily Kimbell (11)	179
Bradley Parker (10)	179

Two Mile Hill Junior School

Jake Morris (9)	180
George Tucker (10)	180
Nathen Scott (10)	181
Ted Yates (9)	181
Urlych Ingabire (9)	182
James Wilmott (9)	182
Melissa Hooper (10)	183
Demi Heaven (9)	183
Josh Selway (10)	184
Saqib Naeem (9)	184
Sam Price (9)	185
Darren Godden (9)	185
Jade Montagna-Malcolm (9)	186
Joshua Grant (10)	186
Mitchell Mainstone (9)	187
Luke Price (9)	187
Brandon Curtis (10)	188
Sydney Barry (8)	188
Nadim Ahmed (9)	189
Liam Wedmore (9)	189
Lucy Lintern (9)	190
Mitchell Tuff (9)	190
Abbie Fish (10)	191
Shannon Davies (10)	191
Elleney Threader (10)	192
Zoe Burchill (10)	192
Charley Millard (11)	193
Joab Magara	194
Bradley Raynard (9)	194
Ellis Fitzgerald (10)	195
Samantha Pomroy (11)	195
Rhiannon Bennett (10)	196
Sania Ali (10)	196
Eilidh Elder (11)	197
George Mattock (10)	197
Tom Willett (11)	198
Emmy Willett (11)	198
Jacqueline Stokes (11)	199
Hannah Smale (10)	199
Hannah Gunningham (8)	200

Nicholas Owen (10)	200
Jake Haskins (11)	201
Laura Bloomfield (11)	202
Jessica Maggs (10)	203
Grace Reed (10)	203
Poppy Hynam (10)	204
Michael Lock (10)	204
Chelsie Bridgeman & Lauren Barnes (10)	205
Karla Dowding (10)	205
Samantha Gould (10)	206
Monique Ash (8)	206
Lauren Preece (9)	207
Daniel Cantle (11)	208
Kayleigh Evans (10)	209

Ubley Primary School

Megan Fowler (9)	209
Charles Mitchell (8)	210
Tom Tarrant (8)	210
Lisa Barry (8)	211
Daniel Stuckey (9)	211
Harriet Walton (9)	212
Henry Chamberlain (8)	213
Juliet Whittam (8)	214
Nancy Inman (8)	215
Harry Chubb (7)	216

Whitehall Primary School

Laura Withey (8)	216
Olivia Thomas (8)	217
Josh Barnett (9)	217
Olivia Collins (9)	218
Alan Gardner (8)	219
Chelsea Owen (8)	220
Chloe Nicholls (8)	220
Brodi Osborne (9)	221
Stefanie Lamch (9)	221
Cristobal Arnaiz (8)	222

Winford CE Primary School
   James Braidley (10)   222
   Thea House (10)   223

: **The Poems**

Winter Wonderland

The frozen winter leaves
Ice crystals violent but smooth.

The slender trees
Powerful with energy.

The hazy landscape of winter
The fluffy flakes fall down to the
Frozen ground.

Snow falls down
A layer over the beautiful aconites of winter.

The sycamore leaves crunchy and cold
The mixture for winter can never be told.

When winter comes
The landscape becomes a winter wonderland.

Donna Janes (14)

In The Snowy Park

The redbreast robins in the icy trees,
The duck pond is icy and sparkly,
The grass is soft and crispy,
I'm cold,
The leaves are soft and white.

Daniel Jones (7)

My Mummy Not Your Mummy (Or A day In The Life Of Twins)

In the morning I'm first to climb out of bed
My brother's still sleeping, he's a lazy-head
Mum calls us to breakfast and when we sit down
The Coco Pops fly and Mum gives us a frown.

We tie up our laces and put on our packs
Which always hang heavy, dropping from our backs
We run fast together, while Mum falls behind
At the school gates she tells us 'You're twins. So be kind!'

But in school it all changes, we go our own ways
We join different gangs and different games play.
My brother will tease me and I tease him back
But *all I feel like doing* is giving him a *big whack*.

The bell rings, it's 3.15. It's time to run back home,
We've got to do our homework, we both let out a groan,
But soon we're busy fighting for the precious TV control
And finally agree on football - yes, Beckham's scored a goal!

It's evening now and our pets have all been fed
We've washed our teeth and faces, and are climbing into bed
When we're all tucked up and warm inside there's a funny game we play
As Mum kisses us goodnight each one of us will say,

'My mummy, not your mummy' . . .
'No! My mummy, not your mummy'
And Mum will laugh and smile
'I'm both of your mummies, and Mum to you both, you were born only minutes apart!
Now go to sleep please and *no more talk,*
Tomorrow's an early start!'

Floren Scrafton (10)
Ashley Down Junior School

Uncle

Dear Uncle,
How I miss you so
When you died, I really didn't know,
Until in the morning,
Everyone was reassuring,
I couldn't believe it, I started to cry,
And why did he have to die?

At first I was really shocked
It was like every answer to my questions was locked.
We went downstairs,
Everyone was so upset,
My mum, my dad, my sister too,
But my baby sister didn't really know you.
As the days went by the funeral came,
When I saw your face I cried even more,
I just wanted you to get up and walk through the door,
But as the years went by, I didn't start to cry,
Now I know I'll just have you in my memories . . .
For centuries.

Lateefah Ngozi (10)
Ashley Down Junior School

Disneyland

I'm going to Disneyland, don't worry I don't need a hand,
I've put all my luggage in my case, a pair of joggers for a race,
A little light for when it's dark,
and fun, fun, fun with a swinging park.
All together is what I need,
for a holiday indeed, now we're arriving at the airport,
It's really not what I thought, thought, thought,
Now we're on the plane, so high, surrounded in the blue, blue sky,
Now we're here in Disneyland, I told you I didn't need a hand!

Billie Skuse-Denley (9)
Ashley Down Junior School

Don't Cry

Don't cry,
I won't die.
Do not fear,
I am here.

Please pray every day.
For me,
For me.

The day I found the one I loved,
Love flew to me like a dove.
You will always be in my heart, in my mind,
And in my grave.
So do not cry,
I will be back.

Fionn McMahon-Parkes (10)
Ashley Down Junior School

Football Crazy!

Football is my favourite sport,
I play it on a court . . .
Weather hot, weather cold,
Weather hairy, weather bold,
Weather snowy, weather rain,
Football never brings me pain.

I play football all day long,
Sometimes even singing a song.
I play it in my Arsenal kit,
Running around makes me fit.
I love football, it brings me luck,
Better than a rubber duck.

Lawrence Hewlett-Walker (10)
Ashley Down Junior School

My Dog

I love my dog,
He did not fetch.
He was not a food hog.
He was gentle and kind,
It slipped my mind.
Oh why oh why did,
He have to die?
I was crying in bed,
To me in my head,
He isn't dead.
He did not chase cats,
He never liked dog Xmas,
Rudolph hats.
You see he was not like other dogs.
He liked mogs.
It's a really sad thing,
It really does sting,
It breaks my heart,
Now we're apart.
Did he have to
Die?

Jasmine Manson (11)
Ashley Down Junior School

Explosion

Over blasting
Over classing
Very bright
Big light
Sparkly silver
Chalky powder
Flies like a kite
Fiery at night
What am I?

Mattias Tamar-Gill (9)
Ashley Down Junior School

The Runaway Homework

Dear Miss,
Just to say all my homework ran away.
I know perfectly well it isn't right
I shouldn't have left it out of my sight.

The fact of the matter is you see
I fell off my chair and hurt my knee.

It was on the table, next to the pen.
But I was called away by my brother Ben.

Next thing I knew it was in the dog's mouth
And I saw him taking it to his doggy house.

When I got there it was torn in shreds,
Just as I was told to go up to bed.

And then this morning I woke up at eight,
And by that time, I was going to be late.

I meant to do it Miss, I really did.
Please don't think that this is a fib.

Lauren Russ-Constant (10)
Ashley Down Junior School

He's Not There Anymore

The sticks he liked I cannot throw
The way he used to eat,
The nice warm bed he used to snuggle up to
Is just an old worn out seat.
The bag of treats I used to give him
Are all mouldy and dry
Everytime I look at them they make me want to cry.
He's not there anymore.

Elle Douel (10)
Ashley Down Junior School

The Truth About History
(Author's Note: Everything in the brackets is (probably) true)

In ten sixty-six,
An arrow in the eye
Killed King Harold.

(It was probably a sword,
Actually.)

In sixteen hundred and five,
Guy Fawkes was arrested
For trying to blow up
The houses of Parliament.

(But it might
Have been a plot
To make the king unpopular.)

In the reign
Of Queen Victoria,
The queen always said,
'We are not amused.'

(Oh no
She didn't.)

In two thousand
And four
Plans to
Demolish the school
Were scrapped

(Which is true.
Unfortunately.)

Chris Maddix (10)
Ashley Down Junior School

Where's Papa?
(In the style of 'What Happened To Lulu?' by Charles Causley)

Where's Papa Mother?
Where's Pa?
Why in the ditch,
Is our own blue and white car.

Why in the driver's seat?
All that we see
Is an overall coat
And below our old house key.

Why is there an empty wallet
There on the floor,
A smashed window
A dented door?

I woke and heard,
A crash outside our car park.
Voices,
Running footsteps in the dark!

Why do you hide away Mother
Why do you look out far?
What happened to Papa Mother?
What happened to Pa?

Ana Ryan Flinn (9)
Ashley Down Junior School

Fireworks

Fireworks are bright
Fireworks are light
Fireworks are colourful
Fireworks are beautiful
I like fireworks a lot you know
I have fireworks on birthdays
But I love the sparklers the most
Remember always have gloves on!

Lorna Besley (8)
Ashley Down Junior School

Names

Names, names, how I forget
Sam or Sally or Auntie Bet
Brother Bob and cousin Joe
All the rest I really don't know.

Was it Mabel, was it Mo or was it Dan
Who liked cookie dough?

Please help me I'm losing it now
I can't even remember the name of my sow.

Was it Susan or was it Mike or was it Louise
Who wanted a bike?

That's the end
I know what a shame!
But I'll write you another one
And what was your name?

Christine Howie (10)
Colston's Girls' School

Family

Old and grumpy
Young and smart
Some are couch potatoes
Some are dainty and bright
Some like me are cheeky monkeys
Running around with glee.

Fat and podgy
Thin as a stick
Burning up calories just like a wick
Charging down the corridor
Bolting down the stairs
Sitting at the table all in pairs,
Sometimes my family make me really mad,
But now I come to think of it without them I'd be sad.

Claudia Lowe (10)
Colston's Girls' School

The Wolf

Teeth sharp, teeth strong
Coat thick, coat long,
I want my cubs to survive and see
That humans are the enemy,
One cub is called Razor
The other called Sting,
I am called Fear as bold as a
King!

We will hunt you
If you hunt us,
We won't harm you
If you won't harm us.
Grey wolves are quite gentle
And loving
And cute,
But beware if you hunt us
We will hunt you too.

You fear our teeth
You fear our claws,
You want our fur to
Hang on your walls, I have told you once
I will tell you again,
Beware of our teeth
Beware of our claws.

Kathryn Parker (10)
Colston's Girls' School

Zebras

Z ebras
E agerly running across the savannah
B ringing their young with them
R acing from the lions
A ntelopes darting from the river
S lowly the zebra falls asleep until the morning.

Sophia Malik (10)
Colston's Girls' School

Roast Dinner

I love to go to Gran's house
On a Sunday after church,
And yet again to my surprise
Upon the dinner table lies,
A huge roast chicken
Plump and round,
That is what I have found.
Neatly peeled roast potatoes,
Gravy that splatters on my nose,
Stuffing balls warm and brown,
Brussels sprouts that make me frown,
Yorkshire puddings gold and crispy,
Lettuce leaves, ends all wispy.
That is what I'll eat for dinner -
I'm not assured it will make me thinner!
Oh lighten up it's a tasty roast
The thing you get at Gran's house
On a Sunday after church,
All piled high upon your plate
Like teacakes at a garden fête!

Laura Sinclair (10)
Colston's Girls' School

Horrible Homework

H orrible homework has struck again
O h what a drag, oh what a pain
M um makes me do it and so does Dad
E astEnders missed, this makes me mad
W hen will it stop? It's eating me alive
O h how I wish my friends would arrive
R un away, run away don't let it get you too
K ick, kill, horrible homework, will you?

Alannah Black (11)
Colston's Girls' School

First Thoughts

After you're born,
There's nothing to do
You just sit in a pram,
Going goo goo goo.

People come and stare,
Poke me and hoot,
Then say something silly like
'Ahh isn't she cute.'

What's that supposed to mean?
Have I gone green
Or am I some sort of
Talking machine?

Is this how I'm going to
Live all my life?
In this stuffy room
That they call nice!

Rachel Quaife (10)
Colston's Girls' School

We Are All The Same!

We are all the same
Black or white
Tall or small
Scared of heights.

We are all the same.
We're part of one big family
So let's all get on in life
And live in happy harmony.

We are all the same
We are part of one big family
I know who I am *Me, Me, Me!*

Paris Olivia May Vassell (11)
Colston's Girls' School

A Jungle Poem

A tiger roars all night
Gives animals a fright
He wants to eat
Lovely fresh meat.

An elephant stomps around
Moving the ground
He likes water to spray
The trees are its prey
He covers half a kilometre each day.

A snake slithers on the trees
Where there are lots of leaves
It has a deadly bite
It hunts the prey in the night
The snake has scaly skin
Which is strong and thin.

A panther jumps up the trees
The panther is three
The panther is an elegant creature
It should be a teacher!
The panther has soft fur
But does not purr
Nor does he stir.

Antonia Self (10)
Colston's Girls' School

SOS

H ow will we get out of here?
E mergency! We're stuck on this island!
L ord, save our souls!
P rayer? It won't work, but . . .

U p above! Look! Up there is a helicopter
S aved! Warm and toasty, smothered in blankets.

Corinne Walker (10)
Colston's Girls' School

Reflections

Wake up, get dressed,
Look in the mirror,
Hair a mess.
Scoff breakfast,
Brush teeth, pack bag,
Walk down the street.
Late for school, teacher's cross,
Do the work, lunch is broth.
In the cloakroom, re-do hair,
Look in the mirror, who is there?
Bell rings, pack bag,
Listen to the teacher nag, nag, nag.
Hurry home, eat dinner,
Have a bath, look in the mirror.
Brush hair, fold the sheets,
Get into bed, sleep, sleep, zzzz!

Josie Pearson (11)
Colston's Girls' School

My Shadow

My shadow follows me everywhere
It reflects along the floor
When I move it's there behind me
Following me everywhere.
Big, doomy and dark
When it suddenly appears
When I touch it, it disappears
It will be back.
But!
I wonder where it's gone?

Frances Nelson (10)
Colston's Girls' School

Fiery Creatures

D ancing, daintily, defiantly, desperately
R unning, racing, resting, reluctantly
A rguing angrily
G runting, gruesomely
O nly
N ice when
S leeping softly.

Charlotte Head (10)
Colston's Girls' School

My Noisy Dog

My noisy dog barks at the birds,
My noisy dog barks at the sheep,
He's busy, loud and very annoying,
As annoying as my baby brother,
But I feel lucky to have a dog.
My dog is actually very sweet,
He's just my noisy, barking dog!

Georgiana Ward (10)
Colston's Girls' School

Witches

W itches gather in their great, grand hall,
I n secret they brew potions, big and small
T hey despise all wizards, goblins, trolls too
C an you hear them cackling? Cackling down at you!
H ave you seen their faces? All slimy and all green!
E very one is so grotesque! And they're so, so, mean!
S ilently they swoop, so quiet they can't be seen!

Isabella Baldo (11)
Colston's Girls' School

The Butterfly

It perches on a leaf
Waiting to take off
Looking all around
Sensing every sound.
Suddenly he spies a bee
Buzzing by a chestnut tree.
Is he looking for his hive?
Presently he takes a dive.

The butterfly remains
Waiting to take flight.
When a lively ladybird
Came zooming into sight,
Small, red, round and bright,
Settling in a cosy spot ready for the night.

Emily Hurse (10)
Colston's Girls' School

Snail's Pace

S low, solid, sulky like,
N ever fast, want to make their journey last,
A lways on the go, though;
I nstant food,
L ovely leaves
S till slow.

P oor pace,
A n endless race,
C an't go fast,
E ver slow.

Ebony Jarrett (10)
Colston's Girls' School

Lions

Lions are scary
    Lions are big it seems to me.
        They are also quite hairy
    And bigger and scarier than a flea.

Lions go hiding in the grass
        Silent as a mouse.
                They watch their prey
Until it's time to pounce.

We see him at the zoo in his cage
    He looks a bit sad, seems to groan,
        But I am not at all sure
I should like to take him home!

Kate Glynn (10)
Colston's Girls' School

My Garden

My garden is behind my house
Small, green, beautiful
As colourful as a paintbox
As pretty as a peacock
It makes me feel happy just looking at it
As happy as a smiling face
As cheerful as a bunch of flowers
My garden
Reminds me that things grown at home
Grow beautifully!

Shelley Silvester (11)
Colston's Girls' School

Nobody's Perfect

A girl once described her brother.
She said:
  B oisterous and noisy,
  O riginally was a bird with a tiny brain
  Y ikes! He put a spider in my bed
  S tupid! Why did God make boys?

A boy once described his sister
He said:
  G etting her own way as usual
  I nquisitive? Yes, always sticking her nose into things that don't concern her
  R ebels until she gets what she wants
  L oves me? Pretends to when adults are about . . .
  S tupid! Why did God make girls?

Beth Norman (11)
Colston's Girls' School

My Pack Of Dogs

My dog Daisy
Likes to hang around with Maisy.
My dog Jess,
Likes eating cress.
My dog Sam,
Is very fond of jam.
My dog Pete,
Has got smelly feet.
My dog Joe,
Likes me saying *'No!'*

What a lot
Of fussy dogs I've got!

Yasmin Kingdon (10)
Colston's Girls' School

The Polar Bear

The silky smooth fur of a polar bear
Is swaying in the breeze
As she cuddles up to her cub at night
It rests upon her knees
Before they know it, it's morning
And the sun again will rise
Making all the polar bears
Feel warm and cosy inside.

Chantelle Sims (11)
Colston's Girls' School

Fictional Fantasies

A witch on a broomstick,
Her cat at her side.
Up hill and down dale,
The wicked pair glide.

In a cave, by a mountain,
Far away,
Is a dragon, all alone,
So they say.

Ogres and giants,
Huge and vast,
They live in castles,
With towers like masts.

Fairies and pixies,
In the moonlight they dance.
While trees stand tall,
Like a knight with a lance.

But do they exist?
Are they real?
Fantasies fly,
Like a wriggly eel.

Amy Spreadbury (10)
Colston's Lower School

The Highwayman Rap
(Based on 'The Highwayman' by Alfred Noyes)

The highwayman was riding
And on his horse was hiding
And in the rain
And down the lane
He came across an old inn door.

Had a bunch of lace at his chin
And breeches of brown doe-skin
The feathers on his hat tonight
Were designed to give everyone a fright.

Over the cobbles his horse clopped
And on the window his fist knocked.
But at this time of night, all was barred and locked
He tapped on the pane
And his girlfriend came . . .

Andrew Fowles (10)
Colston's Lower School

Miss Fairy

At the end of the street lives little Miss Fairy,
With her little old shop, sells anything flary.

From rosy red ribbons, and lacy cravats,
And babies bonnets to tall top hats.

'This looks nice, now try this frock,
I'm awfully sorry, I'm out of stock.'

'Oh, pink my dear, looks lovely on you,
Oh no, I'm sorry, how about . . . blue?'

'Blah, blah, blah, and such and such'
'Ooh, I hope I haven't charged too much.'

And that, my dears, is little Miss Fairy,
With her little old shop, that sells anything flary.

Emma Fredericks (10)
Colston's Lower School

The Highwayman
(Based on 'The Highwayman' by Alfred Noyes)

The wind blew strongly through the trees,
The moon shone brightly on the seas,
The highwayman came out of the night,
On his horse he looked a fright.

His hat was French he'd lace at his chin,
His coat deep red, his pants doe-skin,
His pants were tight, his boots were high,
His pistols sparkled under the sky.

Over the ground he went up to the old inn door in the yard,
He tapped with his whip but it was locked and barred,
He whistled to the window but who was there?
Bess was there with long black hair.

In the dark a stable door creaked,
Tim the ostler listened his face was so peaked,
His eyes were hollow, his hair was mouldy hay,
Dumb he listened and heard the robber say.

'Kiss me Bess, I'm after a prize tonight,
I'll be back with the gold in the morning light,
If they chase me and force me to hide away,
I'll be back by moonlight at the end of the day.'

Benjamin Moore (9)
Colston's Lower School

A Robin

A robin is not just a bird
It is a red apple ripe and round
It is an eagle flapping its mighty wings
It is an aeroplane in flight as it swerves through the trees
A robin is lots of things
But can you find something it's not?

C J Adams (10)
Colston's Lower School

The Highwayman
(Based on 'The Highwayman' by Alfred Noyes)

The wind blew on that dark night
The clouds drifted past the moon so bright
The road glistened like silver over the moor,
The highwayman arrived at the old inn door.

A hat on his forehead, some lace worn with pride,
His coat of red velvet, his trousers of hide,
He looked so smart with his boots so high,
His sword twinkled in the moonlit sky.

The horse's hooves clattered on ground,
He tapped the shutters, but there was nobody around,
He raised a note at the window and knew who was there,
Bess the landlord's daughter, plaiting her long dark hair.

A creaking sound was heard, in the old inn yard,
A man called Tim was hiding, his face white and hard,
His eyes full of anger, his hair like rotting hay,
Silently he sat and heard the robber say:

The highwayman asked for a kiss, a fortune he foretold,
He said he'd be back by dawn break, with the yellow gold,
'If I don't succeed and they chase me through the day,
I'll come back to you at nightfall, let nothing get in my way.'

Jacob Nowak (9)
Colston's Lower School

The Seaside

The sea is calm,
Sand-hoppers crawling over my feet.
The boats look as if they are flying in mid-air.
I hear the stones crawling with the sea
And the sunset begins.
The sea flows away from me
So it is time to go home.

Alex Denton (7)
Colston's Lower School

The Sweets Won't Rot Your Teeth Spell

Rabbits' toenails in the pot
Lots of ants tiny as a dot
Tiger eyes turn round and round
Put the bat in off the ground.

Potion mix potion twirl
Mix and match for a little girl.

Mix the rotting smelly sock
With a bushy tail of a fox
Sprinkle in some witches' powder
The thunder will roar even louder.

Potion mix potion twirl
Mix and match for a little girl.

Take your grandad's false teeth
Get the beef from underneath
Put some spiderwebs in the mix
Now the potion weighs a ton of bricks.

Potion mix potion twirl
Mix and match for a little girl.

Now rub this potion on your teeth
Don't forget you can eat lots of sweets.

Kayleigh Pincott (9)
Colston's Lower School

The Day I Turned Into A Bird!

One morning when I woke up I was in a mess
I wasn't in my bed I was in a nest!
My beautiful skin was feathers, my nose was now a beak!
And outside I heard my family going 'Tweet, tweet, tweet!'

Ellie Diamond (9)
Colston's Lower School

Highwayman Rap
(Based on 'The Highwayman' by Alfred Noyes)

On a dark and windy horrible night,
The pale full moon was shining bright
Riding quickly over the moor,
A highwayman reached the old inn door.

With a French hat sitting on his head,
And a velvet coat that was blood-red.
Legs in breeches of soft doe-skin,
And pistol and rapier twinkling.

At the inn-yard noisy and dark,
Whip on shutters, leaving its mark.
Soft whistle to the window in the sky,
To Bess - beautiful black hair and eye.

Tim listened, his face all white,
It gave him quite a horrible fright,
To hear what the robber said on that night,
That he'd come for Bess before morning light.

He found he could not reach her hand,
So she released her hair from its band.
As the black mass fell over his chest
He kissed it, and galloped over to the west.

Jack Willson-Patel (9)
Colston's Lower School

The Snail

S lithering along like an injured snake
N ever stopping to have a break
A nd always trying to succeed
I t never wants to lead
L onely and silently it makes its success.

Jon Roper (9)
Colston's Lower School

When My School Changed Into An Ocean Liner

It was a usual day at school;
We worked, played and refreshed ourselves until,
I looked out a *porthole!*
The corridors were decked, the playground grass was a deck,
it was like a ship and there was water all around me.

It feels lovely to sail on a deep blue ocean of beautiful fish,
Blue ones, green ones and silver ones.
Mrs Aspden is a captain and the staff are crew members,
Out of the porthole, I saw exotic birds.

I was hungry and went down to the caféteria,
To find a huge banquet of fresh fruit, delicious turkey
And for the vegetarians there were veggie sausages and
fingers with the ripest vegetables.

Suddenly it all whooshed away and my normal day
was normal again . . .
Apart from the debit for daydreaming.

Samuel Miller (9)
Colston's Lower School

Sea Creatures

The fish glide through the sea.
As I watch them go by,
I see the white horses crashing on the seashore
I watch the rocks banging on rock pools
I gaze at the rainbow high in the sky.
The sand is hot
I find a shell that is deep red.
I look in one of the rock pools.
I see lobsters, crabs, urchins, sea snails and lots more.
I go into the sea,
And in the distance I see a flying fish coming towards me.
I also see a dolphin coming as well.

Harrison Ball (7)
Colston's Lower School

Autumn

A purple haze
Enfolds a valley
Beautiful.
There is a light mist hanging above
The mountain's
Leaves scattered on the ground
like a carpet.
A little way off,
There is a patch of scarlet pimpernels,
And some have gaudy cabbage flowers.
I look into the bright blue sky,
Little white clouds all fluffy and small
There is an early morning breeze in the air,
Green fields all around me.
The leaves are gold, red, crimson and green
and yellow!
The dawn has just started,
The sun is just breaking through the clouds
And the first rays of the sun are poking through
the clouds.
I stroll through crispy leaves.
It is autumn!
The sun's going down.
Bye-bye leaves
Till another day!

Isabelle Webb (7)
Colston's Lower School

My School

A lex is my cousin
B en always passes the ball
C ameron is one of my best friends
D on't tell Callum I told you all
E very person in the school
F lies like birds in the Mall
G reg is a boy who likes to shout
H urries home when school is out
I like to rush to get out to break
J asmin is a girl who likes to eat cake
'K ick the ball' says Mitchell Wait
L ike David Beckham at Ashton Gate
M y friend James is really fast
N ever has he come in last
O liver likes to play around
P eople like Oliver's pounds
'Q uiet' says Mr Stock
'R eally now you shouldn't mock.'
S am is hiding under the desk
T ired so he is having a rest
U p and down goes Harry's leg
V ery close to Christian's peg
W hat happened to Jack at the pool?
X -rays showed he couldn't go to school
Y esterday I got a credit
Z ippee I'm glad it wasn't a debit.

Harry Ford (8)
Colston's Lower School

When Snow Tasted Like Ice Cream

I watched the weather forecast this morning
It was supposed to be sunny and warm
When I got to school that day
There was a grey sky and it was freezing.

Then it started to snow, I said, 'Let's make a snowman'
My friend put her head up in the air and opened her mouth
She said, 'Yum this tastes good.'
It tasted of yummy strawberry ice cream.

I thought she was joking at first so I tried a bit
I put my head up in the air and opened my mouth
It really was ice cream, it was strawberry, yum, yum, yum.
It tasted yum.
I was so chuffed, I licked every bit.

Georgina Morrison (9)
Colston's Lower School

The Day We Went Sailing

Today I woke up and found
There were portholes, instead of windows
And ships instead of buildings next door!

In school, Mrs Whitaker was gone
And a cabin-maid was in her place
Instead of corridors, we had decks!

There was a sparkling blue ocean
Where the playground used to be
And instead of Mr Truscott there was a captain!

Mum and Dad weren't in the kitchen,
They were fishing
And looking at the ocean!

Isabella Yaxley (8)
Colston's Lower School

The Beach

On the beach I can see vans selling ice cream
Ice cream is nice and cold
Cold on the beach with the wind
Wind makes the bodyboards go fast
Fast bodyboards go past you
You have to run on the hot sand
Sand is there to make sandcastles
Sandcastles to play
Playing with my friends in rock pools
Rock pools have mussels, crabs, seaweed
Seaweed is bubbly
Bubbles are in the sea
Sea is full of fish
Fish are common in Padstow
Padstow is where people go crabbing
Crabbing takes a long time to do
Doing no work all but playing on bikes
Bike rides go along the beach
Beaches have some caves
Caves have signs because it's dangerous
Dangerous cliffs that you are not to climb on.

Greg Herbert (10)
Colston's Lower School

Invisible

When I go to school, I expect a friend to be with me.
Except they are always playing tag being busy as can be.
When I ask them to come with me
They just ignore me and go for tea.
Until one day, not long ago, a teacher said to me,
'Put on a smile, don't be a while
Then may be you will be seen.'
And from that day on I was!

Georgia Masters (9)
Colston's Lower School

My Family

My uncle . . .
    Tall and thin,
    Stretching out like a slimy snake.

My dad . . .
    Strong as a rock,
    Scary like a monster.

My gran . . .
    Appearing to be wealthy,
    Sitting upon high like a grand queen.

My mum . . .
    Looks posh like Madonna,
    Owning a bit of land.

My brother . . .
    Appearing to be strong,
    Like an ageing gorilla.

My sister . . .
    Loud like Tarzan
    Screams the place down.

Danielle Anderson (9)
Colston's Lower School

My Daddy

If he were a chair he would be a leather back rocking chair.
If he were a time of day it would be bed time.
If he were a holiday he would be a relaxing time on the beach.
If he were a colour he would be a warm colour.
If he were a city he would be Los Angeles with very fast cars.
If he were a drink he would be Stella Artois.
If my dad were an item of clothing he would be a warm jumper.
If my dad were a singer he would be *Eminem*.
If he were a sport he would be rugby.

Ben Woodward (9)
Colston's Lower School

The Snail

Snails are slow,
graceful in their movements.
They go not angrily but calmly,
looking for their food.
Flowers, leaves, the odd herb,
anything like that will do.
The snail's slimy tail
shiny as a washed car.
Now near is night,
the snail can go and feed.
We say goodbye to the snail,
let it go on its travels.
Goodbye little snail,
may we meet again?

Emma Poole (9)
Colston's Lower School

Milo And Trix

Milo
His paw is as big as a tennis ball.
His ear is the softest thing you would feel.
His tail is as long as a man's finger.
His leg is as big as a boy's arm.
He runs as fast as lightning.

Trix
Her hair is as curly as a curled up snake
She swims like a slimy slippery seal.
She eats like a snorting pig.
She snores like a sleeping rhino.
She jumps like a leaping kangaroo.

Alex Wakley (9)
Colston's Lower School

Please

'Please can I go to the toilet Miss,
I've been wanting to go all day
Sir didn't let me go in maths
Neither Miss in French
I'm bursting Miss, please can I go?

Please can I go with Aisha, Sir,
I want to go with her now.
My mum said I should go with her,
Even though she doesn't know Aisha.
Please can I go with her Sir?

Please can you help me Miss,
I've been on this sum for nearly an hour
Even though the lesson is thirty minutes,
I really can't do powers
Please can you help me Miss?

Please can I have a go on the computer Sir,'
'But I thought you needed the toilet girl.'
'I don't need it now Sir, not anymore.'
'Well I suppose you can have a go on the computer girl!'

Olivia Powell (10)
Colston's Lower School

How To Make A Bird

Black eyes like beads, as black as tar.
Feathers as soft as silk and as brown as a twig.
Flying as fast as an eagle, eating flies as small as fleas.
Singing as loud as a cockerel.
A beak like a thin piece of rope
And legs like wire!

Claire Aldridge (9)
Colston's Lower School

Nits!

It's happened before,
Now they're coming back for more.
You bring your child home,
When something catches your eye.
In your child's head of unruly hair,
There's something lurking under there!
It's happened before.
Now they're coming back for more.
It's crawling slowly on their hair,
You'd better hope it's a piece of fluff.
Yet it's small and white,
And is in mid flight!
It's happened before,
Now they're coming back for more.

It really is the pits,
Enough to give you fits!
Haven't you guessed it,
It's *nits!*

Kerala Drew (10)
Colston's Lower School

The Hamster And Squirrel
(Inspired by 'The Owl & The Pussycat' by Edward Lear)

The hamster and the squirrel went to Rome
In a multicoloured jet.
They took some garlic and plenty of Daleks
Wrapped up all ready for the bet.
The hamster looked to the stars above
And sang to a full grown double bass.
'O lovely squirrel, O squirrel my love,
What a beautiful squirrel you are.
You are.
You are.
What a beautiful squirrel you are.'

Adam Rivers (9)
Colston's Lower School

School Time

I arrive at school at eight o'clock,
A pencil case and only one sock,
In my lesson, messing about,
The inevitable comes, a very loud shout!
'Be quiet!' the teacher he screams,
His trousers buckling at the seams.
Lunchtime comes in a flash,
Cottage pie and some mash,
Just smelling the food made me sick!
'Disgusting, repulsive, horrible!' says Nick,
'Lovely food!' says a greedy Rob,
Shovelling it into his big, fat gob.
In the lessons, boring as ever,
Lessons fun? Ever . . . never!
Writing stories supposed to be fun?
I'd rather be shooting myself with a gun!
I arrive home at the end of the day,
Up to my room, but not to play,
Homework still there looking at me,
You may have noticed something, you see . . .
It's not the school that I don't like,
It's a teacher, whose first name's Mike,
When I ask him, 'Can I play?'
He looks at me in such a strange way,
The answer always seems to be no,
So off the classroom away I go.
At the weekend, having fun,
In the scorching, midday sun,
Monday, still there waiting for me,
This Monday, I'll be watching TV!

Jay O'Forrester (11)
Colston's Lower School

Typical Teachers

I'm in the cricket team this summer,
And it's weird as I keep on getting dumber,
My DT teacher Miss Da Soura,
Says that I'm just a big old loser,
But I can believe what I want to,
As my teachers say that I'm koo-koo,
I sit in the classroom swinging on my chair,
Whispering to Sam, so see if I care,
I get a lot of detentions from my teacher,
Who always says I'm a famous creature,
She says I should go and live in the zoo,
And live with the cows that say moo moo.
Finally it's time for the hobbies exhibition,
And I'm introducing my famous eating bogey competition.
It's the final day of school,
And the teachers are letting us play in their pool,
But no, not me, I'm not having any fun,
Could it be that I'm so dumb.
It's the final cricket match of the year,
And I'm bowling the ball, oh no so near.
It was the nearest time I got to the wicket,
Oh no, what a shot.
We only lost by one run, which was from the ball that I spun.
So it's the end of eight hours of school,
And now the teachers say I act like a fool.
So maybe I'll think of moving to the zoo,
And live with the cows that say moo, moo.

Robert Eden (10)
Colston's Lower School

The Debate

You can't honestly think to relate,
To this argument, a big debate.
In fact you can't decide at all,
Who to support in this evil brawl.

The governor thinks it should be there,
But really he doesn't care.
He's faced off by Mrs Brown,
She thinks she wears the crown.

All this raging, roaring, calling,
Hitting, screaming, fighting, bawling.
Councillor John thinks he is right,
Bless him - he's not bright.

It's all gone wrong - out of control.
So much for the neat and tidy poll.
I think we should go before it's too late,
We're stuck in the middle of this terrible debate.

I tried to make my brilliant point,
That I thought of in a burger joint.
But what would you honestly do,
Where to put a temporary loo . . .

Christopher Lynden (11)
Colston's Lower School

A Jet

A jet roars like a pride of lions,
it breaks the speed of sound,
with a great *boom!* Like an elephant stomping
the jet flies through the air like a silver dart,
but when it comes to stopping it seems impossible
for this huge jet,
the parachute slows down the jet
like a turtle clawing onto the sand.

Nathan Patten (9)
Colston's Lower School

The Commenter

I leave my comments on the teacher's table,
Comments on stories, poems, even a fable.
The lesson first of all always makes me feel very small.
Addition, subtraction, multiplication,
Yes you guessed it, maths.
My pen or pencil, my pen I took,
And wrote my comments in the book:
'Why should I do this stupid sum?
I'd rather shoot myself with a gun!
Did I tell you, you really are thin, I've even see a thicker pin.'
In this subject I have a memory like a fish,
Yes it is, it's English.
My pen or pencil, my pencil I took,
And wrote my comments in the book:
'What is the point of this rhyme, it is a total waste of time.
You're so dumb, you can't even teach, I'll rather be on a deserted beach'.
This subject is not the best, we always have a stupid test.
Organs, friction, gravity,
Yes, it's silly science.
My pen or pencil, my pen I took,
And wrote my comments in the book:
'Why should I copy this, I think I'll give it a miss?
Did I tell you, you're so fat, yes, you do look like a bat!'
Now I'm left home, all alone,
To play no, I have to do my stupid homework.
My pen or pencil, my pencil I took,
And wrote my comment in the book:
'I'm not doing my homework today, I'll much rather sit and play.'
The next day the teachers all say:
'You are such a naughty child, you really are so wild'!

Dan White (11)
Colston's Lower School

Hearing And Smelling

Hearing: hearing is
the soft sound of the ocean,
the clashes of the sea,
the drops of the rain,
the noises of people,
the clatter of hail,
the laughing of dogs,
the purr of a squirrel,
the cheers of a human being,
the hum of a bee,
the feet of an insect, a fly, a bug
or a beast.
The shouts of a mother or father
The buzz of a fly,
The rustling of the leaves on a tree.

Smelling: smelling is
the lovely smell of
flowers in the sun,
hamburgers on the barbecue,
my mother's roast dinner,
Dad's expensive aftershave
Gingerbread cooking in the oven.

Oreofe Majekodunmi (7)
Colston's Lower School

In The Day And In The Night

In the day and in the night
In the wind, children play.
Birds are in the air, people watching,
In the day.
People fly, fly their courage, fly their knowledge.
In the night.
People rest.
Children about tomorrow.
In day and in the night.
Smells of flowers wisping smell where I dwell.
On the wall people sit watching world get on with time.
In the night people die, die with honour, die after time.
Time kills, time slays, kills my friends, kills my friends,
Kills my foes.
In the end time wins.
In the day and in the night
People grow ever so slow.
Which keeps knowledge go.
In the night
Sapphires gleam in the moonlight.
People sleep wrapped up tight.
There they sleep till morning light.
In the day and in the night people live.

Ian Clark (11)
Colston's Lower School

Television

In my room on a desk
In a corner at the end of my bed
Is a box, shiny, small and black
With a dark glass screen
And a wire at the back.

I look at it when I get home from school,
To help me relax - Simpsons rule!
History things can sometimes be good
And so are other things with lots of food.

There are some things that make me feel glad
And there are some things that are bad or make me sad.

And if I don't like what I see
I pick up the control and then I can be
A dark warrior in the night
Or a stunt driver and give myself a fright
Or an agent on a mission.

    What am I describing?
      My television.

William Philip (11)
Colston's Lower School

My Person

If my person were a chair he would be a very new sofa.
If my person were a time of day he would be a teatime.
If my person were a holiday he would be a holiday
when you could relax.
If my person were a colour he would be black.
If my person were a city he would be New York.
If my person were a drink he would be Coca-Cola.
If my person were a piece of clothing he would be a leather jacket.
If my person were a sport he would be cricket.
If my person were food he would be chocolate cake.
If my person were an animal he would be a kangaroo.

Alex Yuill (9)
Colston's Lower School

The Banger

Two old men sitting in their three-wheeler
Revving their car like a roaring lion hungry for supper.
A squirrel going past swinging on the back of the bike
Firing past like a shooting star.

The three-wheeler came to a halt
Screeching like a sharpening of a knife.
The two men roared with laughter
Sounding like a group of baboons.

Smoke billowed through the engine
Smelling like the burning of rubber.
Dripping oil from the engine
Sounded like the pitter-patter of rain drops.

The two men started to feel warm
Fire creeping under the seat like a worm digging underground.
Jumping out like a monkey swinging from tree to tree
The car blew up like a lightning bolt hitting a power station.

Ben Sullivan (9)
Colston's Lower School

Soldiers

See the soldiers marching into battle
Trooping like an army of ants.
Hear the guns going off
Crashing like doors slamming in the wind.

Watch the tanks move across the plain
Trudging through the mud like giant armoured beetles.
Hear the grenades exploding
Banging like bricks hitting the floor.

See the people dying from bullets
Falling as if they are going to sleep.
Hear the soldiers celebrating
Chanting like an ancient war cry.

Jonathan Lowrie (10)
Colston's Lower School

The Playground

When we go out to play we have
lots of things to say.
We talk about things which are happening
throughout the day.
The playground is so much fun,
especially when all our work is done.
It doesn't matter if it's rain or sun
we still have lots of fun.
Football, rugby, skipping too,
there's so many different things that we can do.
When we hear the bell ring,
it's time to do the next thing.
Back to class we must go,
Come on everybody, off we go.

Max Allen (9)
Colston's Lower School

The Elephant And The Mouse
(Inspired by 'The Owl & The Pussycat' by Edward Lear)

The elephant and the mouse
Went to Barbados
In a beautiful peanut-brown boat.
They took some money and plenty of bunnies
Wrapped up in a really big coat.
The elephant looked up at the moon above
And sang a little tune
'O lovely mouse! O mouse my love!
What an elegant mouse you are!
You are!
You are!
What a beautiful mouse you are!'

Letisha Gollop (10)
Colston's Lower School

I Am Dyslexic Everyone Says

I am dyslexic everyone says
I know I just learn things in different ways.
I remember everything I hear
But I can't write it down as clear.
If only the pencil would write what I told it,
My stories then would be a great hit.
There are lots of children like me,
People must open their eyes and see.
Don't keep giving us a label,
Because we are very able.
We may know more than you,
Some people don't have a clue.
We will get there in a different way
It doesn't matter what you say,
Please make sure you give us a chance.

Constantinos Polyviou (10)
Colston's Lower School

The Champions

The last minute of the game,
Matt Dawson gets out to Jonny,
The crowd are up, they're on their feet,
Will it be a drop goal?
Jonny kicks the rugby ball in the air,
Will the ball fly over the bar?
No one daring to speak,
It's over!
England is happy!
Australians are mad!
Everyone is shouting,
Martin Johnson holds the cup,
We are the champions!

Jack Collins (10)
Colston's Lower School

World Cup Winners

You're in a ruck,
You only need a bit of luck,
The ball is on the green,
You can't wait to fulfil your dream.
You pick up the ball,
And give Jonny a call,
You pass the ball back,
With a lot of slack.

The crowd roars as he passes to Jonny,
The crowd roars again,
As the ball is in the air,
Now it is not long before it's there,
The crowd roars again,
As it glides between the post
Then everybody roared
And it's all over, England has done it,
They have won the World Cup.

Max Tarr (10)
Colston's Lower School

The World Cup

Jonny did the drop goal,
Martin Johnson kissed the Cup,
Mike Cat did a cartwheel
Lewsey almost blew up,
England won the World Cup,
England won the match,
England won the World Cup,
Thanks to Jonny's snatch.
He kicked it up,
It landed on the other side of the post,
The crowd cheered,
England won,
That would be in the Evening Post.

Oliver Philip
Colston's Lower School

The Rugby World Cup

A hush comes over the crowd as people stand and stare
As the ball spins and hits the muddy ground
People cheer people cry
Jonny Wilkinson runs around
Australia down on the ground
As they sigh in sorrow
People jump
People cheer
Twenty seconds
People count
Ten seconds
Five seconds
One second
We have
Won
The Rugby World Cup.

Lottie Davies (11)
Colston's Lower School

Horses

I canter around and up to the jump
He flies through the sky,
And lands with a thump.

We gallop away, hair and mane blowing
Into the distance where the sun is glowing.

We pass through the woods, all lush with flowers,
I could almost ride for hours and hours.
We must hurry back
Before the sun sets,
I am tired and hungry and so is my horse Jet.

Charlotte Hope (10)
Colston's Lower School

My School's Sailing Away!

I was in school, it was one thirty in the afternoon
Suddenly the school turned into a ship.
I couldn't do anything about it.

The windows were portholes, the door had gone!
Instead there was a stairway.
What was happening?

I got on, and was immediately sick.
I wanted to get off, but when I looked over the edge
The land had gone!

Mr Seashore saw me, he was the captain.
I was glad, I liked him, he was kind.
But then something struck me.

Would I ever see Mum again? I hoped so.
As if I was dreaming, the world was turning.
What had happened?

Oliver Denton (8)
Colston's Lower School

The Race

The car rumbles and revs and roars its engine,
As the green light appears,
It smoothly glides deafening your ears,
Trees bend backwards out of its way,
The car slides,
While it glides
It crashes and tumbles,
And with the car, it has a silent crash,
As it burns and burns and burns.

Raymond Hodges (10)
Colston's Lower School

The Dive

I get on my trunks
to hopefully dunk my dad,
like he'd done to me.

There is a diving board,
I saw a cord
so I jumped and didn't care,
I was in the air.

I saw a clump of hair,
which I tried to avoid.
I was annoyed
I thought I was a bird, but I was actually a fish.

I wish I was a bird
I wish,
I wish,
I wish.

Luke Bailey (11)
Colston's Lower School

The Winning Drop Goal

It is extra time
A long way up the pitch
With Dallaglio
Driving like a bull up the field
Then Jonson like a horse
Galloping up the field
Then Dawson with the ball
Who passes to Wilkinson
Who goes for goal . . .
He gets it there
It is all over
For the Aussies
The cup is *ours!*

Aaron Sealey-Grant (11)
Colston's Lower School

Night-Time

Night is to darkness
As daytime is to light
It seems to come upon us
Without much of a fight.

We do need light to go by
Or else we will be stuck
We may bump into everything
If we don't have much luck.

At night strange things will happen
For darkness is another world.
In mist and gloom and total black
Nocturnal creatures are uncurled.

When night's nearly over
And the sun starts to rise,
We all feel a bit happier
As the birds start their cries.

Arun Mali (11)
Colston's Lower School

Spells

A banana's skin
and a rusty safety pin.
A witch's eye!
and a piece of a pie.
A green cup
and a brown pup.
A ring-a-ding bell
and a crab's shell!

Robert Callaway (8)
Colston's Lower School

The Highwayman's Rap
(Based on 'The Highwayman' by Alfred Noyes)

Outside it was cold
And dark I was told.

He came to the inn
Without a din.

He whistled and knocked
And found Bess in her socks.

'I'm off for a prize
But I'll be back in a trice.'

She said she was mine
But Tim was listening all the time.

Sam Crew (10)
Colston's Lower School

How To Behave In School

Throw your rubbish on the floor,
That's the way to behave in school.
Swear to the teacher,
That's the way to behave in school.
Rip the teacher's book in half,
That's the way to behave in school.
Scream in the corridors at the top of your voice,
That's the way to behave in school.
Cut girls' hair off in the DT lab,
That's the way to behave in school.
Hit the teachers in the stomach,
Is that the way to behave in school?

David Attwood (8)
Colston's Lower School

The Weirdest Day Of School

It was the 18th of January
When I came to school.
It got very cold.

It got colder and colder
Then these coloured balls came down from the sky,
It was weird.

Then I noticed it was snowing,
So I said 'Let's make a snowman.'
Everyone said 'Yeah, that's a good idea!'

So we made a snowball
Then I saw people eating it.
So I shouted '*Stop*'
Then I saw it was an ice cream
So I fell for the joke.

Ellie Carder (8)
Colston's Lower School

My Brother's Like A Parrot

My brother's like a parrot
He's a total chatterbox
His bedroom's like a pigsty
And he's got very smelly socks.

My brother's like a holly bush
He's as prickly as my hair
He likes a spot in the garden
And he roars like a bear.

My brother's like a goldfish
He's a good swimmer in the pool
He frightens people being like a shark
But he doesn't like going to school.

Rhiannon Adams (9)
Colston's Lower School

The Day I Became Fat

I was in my bed in a dream
and I was dreaming about ice cream
I was in bed and it was snowing.

The night was over and I was waking up
I was drinking my tea from my cup
I was walking to school in a funny way.

I arrived at school and it was still snowing
Then something started glowing
The snow had become ice cream.

I started eating the ice cream
And that's what happened in my dream
And I became *fat*.

Jay Chauhan (8)
Colston's Lower School

The Seaside

The sea is cold
The sand is warm
Little creatures slither and crawl
The sea crashes upon the rocks
The waves are coming at me
Lobsters snapping
Crabs pinching
The sea is freezing
The shells are scattered all over the sand
Which is tickling as it moves through my toes.
Worms pop up as I walk along the wet sand,
Kites fly in the wind blowing my way
The sun is shining
What a beautiful day!

Jack Digby (8)
Colston's Lower School

My Day At The Weird Zoo

One day I went to the zoo,
The first thing I saw was a kangaroo.
He jumped up really high,
At the top of the sky.

Next I saw a penguin,
On him was a wide grin
Then he jumped into a swimming pool,
And he came out looking really cool.

Then I went to the panda,
Who were eating salamanders.
The panda was really weird,
Fed by a man with a beard.

The day was very weird,
I still remember the man with a beard.
The day was very funny,
Except for the little bunny!

Sara Procter (9)
Colston's Lower School

Friendship

F riends, friends, don't be dumb
R emember we have lots of fun
I n the class or out at play
E njoy each moment throughout the day
N obody should be ever left out
D ay and day when we're all about
S cience, English, French and maths,
H elp us all in our class.
I hope you like this poem so far,
P *lease* Miss give me a star!

James Baber (9)
Colston's Lower School

My Weird School

My weird school
Is so cool,
But today I feel like a fool.

I see a ship,
I see a man eating a chip,
Look he did a flip.

I see twenty-one puppies,
And they looked furry,
It's so sunny.

I see Zack as a labrador
And he's able to open the door,
Kelly's crawling on the floor.

I have a weird school
Normally it's cool,
Otherwise I'm a fool.

Folu Majek (9)
Colston's Lower School

A Fun Place To Be

The seashore is a fun place to be
I play around in the sea.
I love to play with the crabs but
they always grab.
I like going fishing but they
keep on nibbling.
I can't believe they're so fast,
I really have to cast.
I love to play in the rubber dinghy
till my mum calls me for tea.

Ronnie Arathoon (8)
Colston's Lower School

Night In My Field

Night in my field with the
full white moon,
makes the grass and the trees,
silver and grey,
silver and grey.
Ghostly shadows
flitting across the ground,
scared to be seen,
scared to be seen.
Eerie screech of the
hunting owl,
fills the night
fills the night.

Night in my field with a
cloud filled sky,
torch-light dancing
torch-light dancing.
Animals rustling in the
hedges,
with watching eyes
watching eyes,
imagined creatures
looming out of the dark,
ready to pounce
ready to pounce.

Night in my field
ends at last
light returns
light returns.

Steven Hanney (11)
Colston's Lower School

Tigers

Tigers are wild
cats
But they don't live on
mats.
They have orange and black
stripes
But they don't wear
tights.
Tigers are
big
But they don't
dig.
They kill
deer
But they don't shed a
tear.

Alice Harding (8)
Colston's Lower School

Fireworks Night

Evening came darkness fell
Everyone was excited it was going well.
The fireworks started, the children cheered
And the men drank beer.
The women drank wine
But that doesn't rhyme.
Rockets look like tears when they explode
And everyone knows
I have had a good night and I know I will sleep tight.

Ben Helps (8)
Colston's Lower School

Senses At The Seaside

The surfers are surfing in the waves
Their boards on the horizon look out of reach
Nearer and nearer they approach the shore
Soon they come crashing onto the beach.

People are looking in the rock pools
To see if they can catch crabs in their net.
Limpets and mussels and cockles and shells
And all the little fishes sopping wet.

I can hear the children laughing
I feel the sand tickling my toes
I can smell the salty seaweed
I can feel the sun burn on my nose.

Alex Knight (8)
Colston's Lower School

The Jungle

In the distance over there sat a great fat bear
Quick, quick run away look at that gigantic snake
Lions sleeping in the grass
Lion cubs pouncing on each other
Monkeys swinging from tree to tree shouting to each other
The tigers look like they are wearing striped tights
Elephants stamping through bushes and trees
Giraffes not looking where they are going
Kangaroos bouncing like a child on a trampoline
Rhinos charging at each other
Insects flying around.

Maria Jones (8)
Colston's Lower School

The Girl And The Mouse

There was a girl called Lily,
and the mouse was called Billy.
I let him in the house,
He was such a pain, the little mouse.
He went outside,
He felt like he was going to die.
The girl was in bed,
When the mouse was dead.
When she woke up and went downstairs
The mouse was still not there.
So poor Lily
Never had Billy again.

Lillie-Mae Maddox (8)
Colston's Lower School

Apples

Would you like my apple?
This apple is ripe and red.

This apple is shiny,
And shines in the sun.

This apple is so delicious,
And I would eat a hundred.

Apples grow on trees,
In the sun all day.

This apple is so bright,
Would you like my apple?

Anna Thomas (7)
Colston's Lower School

The Sea

The sea is blue,
The sand is yellow.

The shells are opening,
The sea creatures are crawling.

The waves are moving,
The waves are blue.

The octopus is slimy,
The octopus' leg broke.

The fishes are swimming,
The fishes are caught.

The sea is powerful,
The sea keeps lots of secrets.

Eva Polyviou (8)
Colston's Lower School

Poem Of The Seaside

I like going to the beach.
I hear the waves crashing in the sea.
The sea is cold and the sand is hot.
The sea is glowing like a mirror.
In the rock pool I see baby crabs and
limpets that stick to the rocks.
The ice cream van is full of children.
The shops have sold out of buckets and spades.
The beach is covered with seaweed, pebbles and sand.
I love to swim, I love to surf, I love going to the beach.

Joshua Wanklyn (7)
Colston's Lower School

My Snowman

I wanted to have a friend
So I got myself a snowman
I played with him all day
But he never touched the saucepan
I let him sleep with me
After we'd had our tea
In the morning he had gone
After wetting my bed at dawn.

Sandeep Vijay (7)
Colston's Lower School

Windy Nights
(Inspired by Robert Louis Stevenson)

Whenever the moon and stars are set,
Whenever the moon's alive.
All night long in the dark and wet,
A man goes for a dive.
Late in the night when the fires are out,
Why does he swim and swim about?

Alice Fillingham (9)
Coniston Primary School

Windy Nights
(Inspired by Robert Louis Stevenson)

Whenever the sun and clouds are set
Whenever the wind is high
All night long in the horrible and wet
A man goes riding by
Late in the night when the fire's smoulder
Everywhere is looking older.

Jack Trueman (9)
Coniston Primary School

Windy Nights
(Inspired by Robert Louis Stevenson)

Whenever the birds are in their nest,
Whenever the time has come,
The way that he may never rest,
His frozen hands go numb,
He makes the trees blow and swing,
These windy nights blow everything.

Whenever the clocks are ticking at night,
Whenever branches are broken,
All night long the witches fight,
While the man is given his token.
By at a twist he goes and then
By at a turn he comes again.

Leah Tozer (9)
Coniston Primary School

Night-Time Cinquain

So dull,
No noise, silence,
All you see are shadows moving,
The only light, the shining moon,
Day comes.

Zoe Broomfield (10)
Coniston Primary School

Maths - Cinquain

So hard
Add, take away
Multiples and factors
Pencil, pen, protractor; we start
Boring.

Leanne Couchman (10)
Coniston Primary School

Windy Nights
(Inspired by Robert Louis Stevenson)

Whenever the sky is black at night
Whenever the wind is high
To see - there is hardly any light
A man goes riding by.
Late is the night when the fires are out,
Why does he gallop and gallop about?

Stacey Peard (8)
Coniston Primary School

Windy Nights
(Inspired by Robert Louis Stevenson)

Whenever the sky is black like a crow,
Whenever the wind is high,
As he sharply whistles and blows.
A man goes riding by.
Late in the night when the fires are out,
Why does he gallop and gallop about?

Danielle Lock (9)
Coniston Primary School

Windy Nights
(Inspired by Robert Louis Stevenson)

Whenever the sun is lowering down
Whenever the wind is high
As the night wears a frown,
A man goes riding by.
Late in the day when the lights are tired,
Why does he act like he's been fired?

Luke Winchcombe (10)
Coniston Primary School

Windy Nights
(Inspired by Robert Louis Stevenson)

Whenever the sky is velvety black,
Whenever the wind is high,
The trees are busy saying 'crack'
A man goes riding by.

Whenever the moon and stars are set,
Whenever the wind goes by.
All night long in the dark and wet,
A man goes roaring high.
Late in the night when fires are lit,
Why does he gallop bit by bit?

Callan Bourne (9)
Coniston Primary School

Daffodils

The sweet summery smell runs up my veins
While they play in the breeze.
My eyes were amazed at what I saw
Golden daffodils.
I can touch the soft sweet petals.
The clouds float by and shine on me.
Then take the heat off me.

Jack Skinner (9)
Coniston Primary School

Night-Time - Cinquain

Night-time
Creepy and dark,
You may be so frightened
For things that might come back alive.
Beware.

Toni Lawrence (10)
Coniston Primary School

Daffodils

Daffodils are as golden as the sun,
and as silky as the moon.
Daffodils smell like sweets,
I know they will be budding soon . . .

Daffodils - lying under the trees.
Gently dancing in the breeze.
Daffodils swaying under the moon,
as I go they say, see you soon.

Alya Strode (8)
Coniston Primary School

Daffodils

I can hear the beautiful daffodils
But I can't see them.
I can smell their springtime scent
But I can't see them.
Finally I can see their golden-yellow sparkle,
I can touch their soft, yellow hands.
Daffodils come in yellow and gold,
Dancing in the breeze, gently touch the wind.

Daniel Rees (8)
Coniston Primary School

Daffodils

Daffodils are golden-yellow
Daffodils swaying side to side.
You do a sprightly dance
You're the yellowest flower on the land.
You're yellow like the sand
Darting up and down.
Colours, golden-yellow and green.

Lana Skuse (8)
Coniston Primary School

The Daffodils

The daffodils sing and bring summer onto Earth,
The sun rises and summer begins,
The daffodils dance for joy,
As the sun's warmth takes over.
The clouds float elegantly as the breeze blows,
The strawberries and blackberries start to grow.

Zoë Parry (7)
Coniston Primary School

Television - Cinquain

Black screen,
Switch on button,
Fuzzy picture moving,
TV as boring as the rain,
Goes off.

Chelsea Thomas (11)
Coniston Primary School

Valentine's Day - Cinquain

Care, hug
Roses so red
Valentine's Day present
To give your one and only love
Kiss, kiss.

Daniella Prowse (10)
Coniston Primary School

Midnight - Cinquain

Midnight
Dark and lonely
Many people now scared
When spooky creatures come to life
Night falls.

Stacey Coleman (11)
Coniston Primary School

Television - Cinquain

I watch
Television
Wildlife, cartoons and sport
It is my life, no time for tea
Or books.

Joe Shipley (11)
Coniston Primary School

Television - Cinquain

A box
Box with pictures
It hypnotises you
A person with square eyes cannot
See me.

Lisa Coghlan (10)
Coniston Primary School

Star Wars - Cinquain

Star Wars
Is a very
Good film, for people who
Like violence and lots of death
It's cool!

Daniel Harvey (11)
Coniston Primary School

SATs - Cinquain

Sitting
at a table
picking up my pencil
touching paper, pencil snapping
Oh no!

Sacha Ware (11)
Coniston Primary School

Spinners Secret Day

In darkened corners,
It hides there,
Light and small.

Quick and cunning,
Fast and creepy,
Its spindly legs
Light but fast.

Its brownish-blackish
Spiderweb camouflaged.

Jordan Blammon (10)
Fair Furlong Primary School

Spider

In the garden,
In the dark,
You spin the
Pure white webs,
In the night
You will hide
In cracked places while
Shadowed secrets wait.

Black as night,
You shall not sleep,
For webs you spin,
Day will creep.

Day has come,
For all to wake,
It's light now,
For all to see,
The pure white thread,
All around,
The garden is full with
Diamond lace.

Lee Spray (10)
Fair Furlong Primary School

Spiders

Dark and shadowed,
Lace too fine to see,
Hidden a secret,
In boulders and bushes.

Web, web, web?
Where are you?
I'm going to catch my
Prey with you.

Conor Malin (9)
Fair Furlong Primary School

Spinners Web

Spinners web,
Hanging high,
Spinners bed,
Makes them dead.
Flies the prey,
Catch them fast,
That's the day,
They say.
When the frost
Comes by.
The web begins
To say goodbye.

Spinners home,
Shows now,
Flies flown,
Into webs
That makes . . .
Them dead,
On glittering
Webs with dimmed lace.

James Wall (9)
Fair Furlong Primary School

Spinner Spider

Spinner spider you move so fast,
Spinner spider you are a brat,
You swiftly move to your house,
You eat your dinner, it's a louse.

You are so big and black,
Spinner you are so hairy,
You will move again to your house,
Spinner spider you are so scary.

Kieran Giddings (9)
Fair Furlong Primary School

Spider

Out the back,
On the wall,
A spider rakes,
My garden wall.

Spider big looks,
For a home spider,
Small has got one,
He looks in a dark place.

The spider looks for,
A place for its secrets,
He looks in dark and damp,
His secrets are shown.

Leon Dew (9)
Fair Furlong Primary School

Spinner The Spider

Spinner scuttles
Across the floor
Fast and quick
He runs to hide.

His dark black eyes
His hairy scary legs
His big creepy body
Looks for a home.

He finds a crack in the wall
Scuttles through the hole
And he builds his home inside.

Paige Batchelor (9)
Fair Furlong Primary School

Spider

I have a creature,
As black as night,
It crawls very fast,
Spreading diamond thread,
Very quietly and speedily.

Out of the window he'll jump,
Trying to find a secret home,
But when the sun comes out,
His secret will be known.

On a cold and frosty night,
My spider tries to find a web,
He looks at all the dark, damp places,
Now my spider found a web.

In the bright sunny morning,
My spider gets a fright,
Because he knows his secret is known,
Now he's got to find a new home.

Tracy Thomas (10)
Fair Furlong Primary School

Hairy Scary Spider

The hairy scary spider
Was hanging on the wall.

It lives all alone
Inside the phone
It crept across the floor
And scuttled under the door.

He saw a pot of flies
And they tell so many lies.
He drank some cider because
He is a spider.
The hairy scary spider.

Amie Purnell (10)
Fair Furlong Primary School

Spider's Adventure

Across the wall,
Up the tree,
Eyes look left,
Eyes look right,
Find his web,
Day and night.

'Yes my web!' Spider cries,
Tiptoe quietly to the front door,
'Come on in!' my web declares,
'It's your home, come on!'

Swoop onto the cupboard,
Jump to the bed,
Fly to my web,
Flapping my legs to and fro,
'Hooray! I've found my web!'
Spider said proudly.

Heather Milton (9)
Fair Furlong Primary School

Secret Webs

Deep underground,
Dark and damp,
Swiftly it moves,
Across the floor,
Not a sound or a whistle,
Could be heard.

Moonlight was flashing,
Stars were sparkling,
Sun was appearing,
And day begins.

Spider secret known,
When a light appeared,
Across the deep, dark ground.

Khadija Ali Hassan (9)
Fair Furlong Primary School

Spider's Secret

In the garden,
Slowly it scuttled,
Can't be seen,
Rhythmically legs clatter,
And nothing heard.

Night comes now,
All webs hidden,
Nothing is seen,
But a lot heard.

Morning comes now,
Nothing left hidden,
Everything is seen,
Even the webs.

Secrets are revealed,
Webs glisten today,
Spiders gone now,
For new webs.

Kieran Westgate (9)
Fair Furlong Primary School

Spooky Spider

Spooky spider
Crept in the night
And gave a fright.

Spooky spider
Spinning his web
Crept and crept

Find the money spider
Good luck you'll get.

The spider hid behind his web
Waiting for his prey.

Curtis Rush (11)
Fair Furlong Primary School

Spider

Out in my garden,
In the night,
A spider crawls
In the dark,
He moves everywhere,
Across my wall,
Across my shed.

He's found his home,
Now he goes to bed,
Under the bricks,
By my wooden shed,
Unexpected he says . . .
'I'm not going to be disturbed.'

But the sunlight comes,
His secret is known,
His web has really shown,
The web is covered with frost and stone,
And pure white threads,
You see it all,
The garden is filled with diamond lace.

Jack Tucker (10)
Fair Furlong Primary School

The Spooky Spider

The spooky spider creeping through the hall,
Run, run, run, don't you fall.

Here he comes,
Back along the silk road web.

Looking for his treasure
In his golden threads.

Chantell Searle (10)
Fair Furlong Primary School

Spinner's Secret

Alone in the dark,
It's so camouflaged,
As it crawls along,
It's shivering and cold.

Looking left,
Looking right,
But it's hard,
In the night.

It doesn't help,
When he's black,
And then a flicker,
Of the light.

Speedy jump,
Quick and sharp,
The sun disturbs him
As the spider's web
Is shown!

Hayley Delaney (10)
Fair Furlong Primary School

Spider

Spider, spider spin your web
Spider, spider go to bed.
Spider, spider come to me
Spider, spider come to tea.

As the spider sits on his bed
He doesn't know what to say
But falls asleep instead.

When he eats his flies
He wakes in the morning
And suddenly dies.

George Gray (10)
Fair Furlong Primary School

Spooky Spider!

Spooky spider
Spun his web
Crept and crept
Then silently slept.
Find the money spider,
And get good luck
Swift and silently,
The spinner spider sped.

Spooky spider
Made a web,
Stuck his venom
With a sting,
All alone he catches prey,
And all the other insects stray.

James Langridge (10)
Fair Furlong Primary School

Creeping Spider

As the spider lies behind the web,
Ready for food before bed.

Wrapping prey
For food today.

Snuggled in bed
Ready to eat
A fly's head.

Ready for tomorrow
The fly's will end
In sorrow.

Nick Lathrope (10)
Fair Furlong Primary School

Spider Spider!

Spider spider
is so small

Spider spider
fell in the pool

Spider spider
in the loft

Spider spider
come and hide.

Spider spider
a fly has
died!

Ben Yearsley (10)
Fair Furlong Primary School

The Spider's Secret

Cold and dark,
The spider approaches the dark
And gloomy pot

To spin his web,
Suddenly the sky opened up
And started to rain.

The web glistened and the secret was out.
The spider was proud
And he solemnly declared his web
Had been found.

Kirsty Lester (9)
Fair Furlong Primary School

Spooky Spider

The hairy scary spider
wants a drink of shandy
because he got a friend called Pandy
he lives all alone down by the phone.

Darker and darker the room got
the spider crawled across the floor
into the door.

He saw a pot of flies and
they told him a pack of lies.
He ran up the hall
onto the kitchen wall.

Toni Hazell (10)
Fair Furlong Primary School

The Spooky Spider

The spooky spider
Creeping in the hole.
Running through the garden
Running through the hall.

There he is on his eight long legs.
Running up the stairs
And now he fell.

The spooky spider
Going back in his hole
Now we won't see him out at all.

Katie Andow (10)
Fair Furlong Primary School

The Secret Spider

Steady and calm,
Secret and soft
The spider is making his way up to the loft.

His legs are like twigs
His tummy's like a ball
And he's very good at climbing walls.

Cold and gloomy
Creeps across the floor
Steady now spider I think I hear a door.

He looks around the box
And there just in front of him was his prey.

I'm hungry little spider I think it's time for your tea.

Paige Nelmes (9)
Fair Furlong Primary School

The Wife With No Head

Spider, spider, creepy jeepy
He and his mate are looping
And creeping
Then when it is time
They both start sleeping!

When the morning comes
They hear a sound and run!

The spider spins a spindly web
Then he finds a wife with no head!

Creepy!

Shonnie Coles (9)
Fair Furlong Primary School

Weeper

In the dark mist,
Of a cold web,
A spider sat weeping,
Crying, a loss of a wife,
'Why did she have to die alone?'
Wept the poor spider,
Sobbing, tears dripping down,
From his six eyes.

'Horrible humans!'
Said the spider,
'Pink flesh I cannot eat!
Unlike me, black - smooth
- silky!'
The spider sat down,
And pulled out his pipe,
He puffed on it once,
Took it out and coughed.
'Oh, how I miss her'
Our spider blubbed,
'She was so dear to me!
Her beautiful eyes and
Her teeth - perfection!'

The spider snivelled,
Unwedded, unbefriended -
Alone.

Sarah Lane (9)
Fair Furlong Primary School

The Man

The man came, he had a gun
I started to shiver
I heard the gun click like a clock
Bang I felt the bullet in my liver.

Albie Mayo-Hagues (8)
Hillcrest Primary School

The Fairy In Charge Of The Sea

She flies up high
almost skims the sky.

When she is happy she is like the rippling sea
tickling the pebbles on the beach.

When she is angry she pulls up the sea
into a crashing, shrieking wave.

When she is sad the sea is grey
like cold lead.

When she is cheeky the choppy waves chase
each other along the shore.

She falls back down low
so tired so slow.

Anna Jordan (9)
Hillcrest Primary School

The Lie!

Today I said something really mean,
My friend told the teacher then I told a lie,
My teacher said, 'Go and sit in the dark, dingy dungeon'
Then she gave a big sigh!

In the dungeon there was a creepy crawling rat,
Then my tears made a swimming pool because I started to cry,
My face was red as blood,
Then there it was the lie and with him the bad lie.

At night I had a scary nightmare,
Nightmares of a slithery slimy snake,
I was shivering,
Then zoom I was awake.

Safa Iqbal (8)
Hillcrest Primary School

The Sun And Storm

The storm has upset many people
His emotions are his only problems
Everyday he sits
Consuming rage,
The sun won't accept his gift.

This makes Storm mad
Making all his hailstones shatter glass.
All his wind, all his rain
Turning the ocean into white horses.

The sun she gives in
She feels like she's the prey that can't be caught.
She accepted and then,
Only then a rainbow was formed.

Stan Portus (10)
Hillcrest Primary School

School

Nine o'clock on Monday morning,
Everybody comes in yawning.

Maths on Tuesday - worst of all
Why do I have to come to school?

Swimming on Wednesday - it's really great!
I share a cubicle with my mate.

Thursday is the busiest - lots to do!
Assembly, recorder and literacy too!

At last! It's Friday! Hip hip hooray!
We can all go home and play.

Lauren Aquilina (8)
Hillcrest Primary School

Dogs

Dogs run,
Dogs hide,
Dogs bark,
Dogs glide.

Dogs jump,
Dogs leap,
Dogs poke,
Dogs peep.

Dogs trot,
Dogs race,
Dogs eat,
Dogs chase.

Melissa Almeida (8)
Hillcrest Primary School

Dogs
(Based on 'Cats Sleep Anywhere' by Eleanor Farjeon)

Dogs sleep anywhere,
On a table,
On a chair.

In the wash,
Behind the bin,
In the garden,
They always win.

Dogs sleep anywhere,
Any any table,
Any any chair.

Karis Godbeer (9)
Hillcrest Primary School

Seasons

Winter, there's a blizzard,
The cold air is like grit being rubbed into my skin.
The water is turning into ice,
It's getting colder,
I want to go home.

Spring, there are new animals and plants,
It's still raining but it's like warm sand on my face.
The colours of the plants bright pink, vibrant red, orange,
Clear yellow and green leaves,
Can we go to the park?

Summer, the sun is beating down on my bare skin,
The colourful flowers are like windmills in the warm breeze.
The water in the paddling pool is warm
Everyone is outside having fun.

Autumn, the leaves on the trees are falling,
Crispy yellow, orange, red, brown.
It's getting colder,
Everyone's inside drinking tea,
Why can't it still be summer?

Rosy Pearson (10)
Hillcrest Primary School

Teachers

T he school bell rings at 9 o'clock
E choes through the corridors,
A rmed with books,
C arrying boxes,
H elp I just dropped one,
E arlier I heard the teacher roar,
R oar, class has already begun.

Elise McDonald (9)
Hillcrest Primary School

The Chill

Sun saw wind running around,
Causing lots of chaos.
Wind was angry, very angry.
He made everyone shiver when he went past.
Wind passed through everybody.
He soared into the sky,
Flying over to the burning sun
Who was watching him.
Sun's smile turned to ash.
The wind looked like a howling wolf, ready to pounce.
Wind dragged his razor-sharp claws across sun's face,
Sun flinched as fiery fangs slashed his body,
Sun was like a red balloon panting
Letting all his anger out,
Wind plucked his fangs out of sun one by one.
Wind flew away,
Sun was safe again.

Tom Netto (10)
Hillcrest Primary School

Winter Strikes Back

Winter comes swiftly
Through the air howling,
Like a wolf in pain
Just sitting stiff as a dog
On a hot summer's day.

Then suddenly the wind turns
Rapidly, hard as a rock,
Winter turns the window
A pale frosty white
Like a frosty road.

Freezing fog smothers up the cars
They instantly vanish.

Alex Sinclair (11)
Hillcrest Primary School

The Storm

Quickly, but silently the sun slid away
as the angry clouds filled the sky with deep darkness.

The rain brushed the ground's sweeping dirt
and filth to the drains while the wind got ready
to pounce like a furious fierce tiger.

Wind couldn't hold herself back
she roared and came diving down like an eagle
desperate to attack.

Rain washed the Earth with her tears
like her mother grieving for her child's death.

The sky dropped dead as the silence filled the air
like spices warming but bitter.

Rain hid herself over the homes by wrapping herself
in a soft, wet blanket whilst the wind took off
over the clouds looking for a home.

Joanna Hay (10)
Hillcrest Primary School

Hail

Hail was a man who strode powerfully through the city.
As everyone hid for cover,
he spat and threw himself on to the city,
enlarging every second.
He paused and stopped growing.
Hail saw a building and headed towards it.
The building had plummeted to the ground like a bird
being shot out of the sky,
Because hail had caused an ongoing shower of huge hailstones.
Hail was pleased at his destruction.
Ruins caused by hate.
Hail looked back on the town.
An evil grin spread across his bitter face.

Billy Golding (10)
Hillcrest Primary School

Storm Fight

Storm crouched helplessly into a corner,
Wind whipped in and out looking for her.
Everyone knew they were getting closer.
Second after second things were getting tense.
Wind was howling like a wolf.
Storm wished wind would vanish.
Wind turned into storm's corner.
Wind was glad he had found her.
Storm's screeches were like a banshee.
Wind was ready.
Wind was set.
Storm and wind arose into the sky
So high that the heaven's opened.
Rain was falling, sleet and snow.
Colliding
Spinning
A sudden moan filled the sky.
Storm and wind fell to the ground.
Everybody ran for shelter.
Silence . . .

Chelsea Walton (10)
Hillcrest Primary School

Winter

Winter's cold wet teardrops like autumn leaves,
As he swoops past your village
He leaves a snowdrop morning for us to play in.
A blizzard forms, but sun gleams through
Spring arrives, Winter runs away
While the world comes out of hibernation.

James Sharman (10)
Hillcrest Primary School

The Final Bout

Winter lay in wait
listening to Spring charging forth.
Winter ascended into the sky
letting a blizzard loose.
The land turned white
Spring rose
Leaving a trail of golden dust behind him.
He conjured a blanket of warmth to heat the Earth.
Winter created a fistful of wind
And let it rip across the sky.
The wind caused havoc
Blinding everything in its path.
Spring summoned blades of light
Which soared around winter like a flaming phoenix.
Winter howled like a dying wolf
And vanished -
A flower bloomed
Spring arrived.

Harry Cox
Hillcrest Primary School

Storm

Thunder and lightning roar in the sky
Stealing children's hearts
Thrashing everything in their way.

The storm is getting harder
Wind howling like a pack of wolves
Like a lady
A lady crying for help.

The blazing sun comes out
The world is safe for another day.

Sheldon Golding (10)
Hillcrest Primary School

Rain's Howl!

The rain cries as she fills her eyes with tears,
All she hears,
Is the trickle of streams,
And the screeching of the wind,
The rain's voice is echoing in the cold air.

She screams, shouts, scatters the world . . .
With rain,
As she cries in pain,
There's one thousand droplets piercing the ground.

Rain's black dress sways in the wind,
If you make her upset,
She will make a terrible storm,
Rain's life will be turned upside down.

Natasha Morris (10)
Hillcrest Primary School

Wind, Rain And Sun

Wind roared at the rain like a tiger,
Rain drew its claws over the wind,
It was as if they were turning on me,
The rain's droplets felt like sharp knives on my face
And I could hear the wind howling in my ear,
Then everything went silent.
Wind blew soft silk against my cheek,
Droplets gently fell into the palms of my hands.
Everything felt calm.
Wind went cold, my hands were frozen,
Sun came out
Sun felt like my mother holding my hands to warm me.

Eva Freeman (11)
Hillcrest Primary School

Rain

Rain is a person forced to come out
Rain is a person who is lonely and sad
He doesn't mean to hurt
He's just trying to be friendly
Is that really bad?
The rain sounds like the gentle tapping of fingers
When he thinks of the evil sun
He begins to cry and feel safe
How could anyone be so mean but popular?
It's not fair!
When he pours everyone deserts the outside world
Nobody cares for the rain
He wants to catch a train
He feels like a fly you keep flicking away
Rain is a lonely person who doesn't mean to hurt
So remember next time you see the rain
He has feelings too.

Helena Ferguson (10)
Hillcrest Primary School

Ocean

A wave crashing
A tail flashing.

A swift fin
Comes sailing in.

A shark chasing
A flat fish facing

Dinner found
Now homeward bound.

Jessie Greenwood (9)
Hillcrest Primary School

Winter

Winter, the cold perishing days
Winter the night sky
Winter the glacial air on my skin
Cold bitter winter.

Snow, the white blanket on the ground.
Snow, the winter frost on my lips
Snow, the icing across the land,
Cold bitter winter.

Ice, the night sky on the wall
Ice, the chilled rock of the Earth
Ice, the freezing pain on my skin
Cold, cold winter.

Ben Jester (11)
Hillcrest Primary School

Winter

Winter comes once again
The wind sweeps through my hair
As it drifts through the sky
With its angry face
It's like we have done something wrong.

One more blow and the sun will come out
I think to myself
The wind howls with hunger.

Everything goes quiet
I can see my breath in the air.
Like grey smoke spreading
Silently through the cloudy mist.

Emma Cresswell (10)
Hillcrest Primary School

Absent

Still and silently the winter months hush the animals to sleep,
Sun wraps her cloak around herself
Gathering her piercing rays, collecting all the light,
Leaving the wood in darkness until spring comes.

The absence of wind leaves the tree's jagged branches frozen,
The wood remains still
No wind
No rain
No sunshine
Crackling and crunching of boots are like grinding teeth
                                           crumbling into chalk,
Leaves below shatter into tiny pieces.
Silhouetted at the foot of the wood, Wind hovers wearing
                                           a friendly smile

Dazzling a spotlight on his face
Sun giggles
Spring returns.

Ellie Pope (11)
Hillcrest Primary School

Battle Of The Sky

Sun slowly asked storm if it was her day to shine.
Storm denied so he quickly thundered his anger out to Earth.
Sun didn't know what to do and then she thought of what to do
She gave no reply
So she shone
Both storm and sun gave no reply
In shock they saw the biggest rainbow being formed on Earth
None had won
But Rainbow.

Aisha Sahi (10)
Hillcrest Primary School

Strangers

The haunted castle stood on end,
It was dark, deserted and creepy.
The only light was a glimpse of
The moonbeam shining through,
Like a cat's eye.

Then suddenly there were footsteps,
There was a stranger there.
A lifeless, creaky stranger,
With eyes the colour of red blood.

Deadly shadows came from everywhere
The unusual figure crept silently across the crooked floor
With his cloak the colour of dark, sloppy mud and
His teeth the size of sharp *knives!*
Then he said a riddle and vanished
Into the air!
That was the end of him!
Ede Dugdale-Close (8)
Hillcrest Primary School

Changes

Autumn leaves drop like tears.
But Winter's cruel hands start sweeping them back
Locking them in the past,
Though he soon falls to his knees - dying.
A light,
So bright,
Introduces the spring.
Spring grows with hope.
Summer takes over, as cheerful as ever
Like she'd been there all her life
As though nothing had ever changed.
Lily Bland (11)
Hillcrest Primary School

Frosted Flowers

Winter's reign was coming to an end.
Ice melted like stars dripping with fear.
He collapsed helplessly to his knees
Crying as if his hands were tied.

Slowly, surely, one by one flowers
Appeared, opened.
Rainbows coming out to play.
A harsh wind swept through the town
Whispered, 'Spring's here, she's here.'

At the last bed of the frosted flowers
They met
Winter's face, white as chalk,
Spring's a healthy golden glow.
Fireflies danced around the passionate couple.
The sight was an eclipse of colour
That the world will never see again
Then
A
Kiss . . .
. . . And winter was gone forever.

Holly Baker (11)
Hillcrest Primary School

Snake

A snake lies asleep in the grass in a hole.
A vibration!
Suddenly the snake awoke, he stuck out his tongue
And sensed a little mouse.
The snake slithered silently out the hole and bit into the mouse
The poison sank into the mouse and he died.
So the snake slithered into the hole.

Harry Atkins (7)
Hillcrest Primary School

The Silence Of The Night

The silence of the night grew thick
Darkness so quiet
But then the darkness fades into mist
A crash, a bang, and then comes the shadow of light.

The cloak with what appears to be a skeleton inside.
They disappear then appear again but this time I'm surrounded.
They come but this time walking, this time wailing the faint
                                              sounds of death.

Then I wake up in a chamber, a prison.
My dirty clothes were tattered.
I saw skulls on the floor.
Then I saw the bones, no one could help.

I grew older, older than anyone I had heard, seen or known.
I could not die, just suffer.
The years went on, the ground grew mistier.
I found a message in blood and it said . . .
'Goodbye, we were destroyed, if you ever escape darkness will fall!'
This was from the dead guard.
The keys!
Noooooooo
The darkness . . .

Oscar Pope (8)
Hillcrest Primary School

My Mum

My mum is great,
My mum is cool,
My mum likes to go in the swimming pool.

She hugs me when I'm sad,
She kisses me when I'm blue,
Mummy, Mummy, Mummy, I so love you.

Tegen George (8)
Hillcrest Primary School

In My Orange Juice

Autumn leaves, falling from the trees.
Children skipping, with orange ropes.
Orange shoes, on feet.
Orange cars, whizzing past,
Orange people, inside.
Orange, dazzles your eyes.
Orange rock, slowly gets covered,
With green algae.
Hot orange, in a sunset.
Orange bark, falling off onto the pavement.
Orange, striped tigers.
Orange, striped tigers,
Stalk orange toffee in orange grass
All in my orange juice!

Anna Fleming (8)
Hillcrest Primary School

Hunting

          In a dark hole,
        The snake's
      Asleep.
        He feels
            a vibration.
              He glides
                  gracefully
                      along the
                  grass.
              He spots
            the prey,
        Gulp!
      The prey is
    swallowed.

Dexter Doling-Baker (8)
Hillcrest Primary School

Orange Poem

Orange is the burning light
Of a tiger crawling in grass.

Orange is the ringing phone
Made by the Orange phone company.

Orange is the sunshine
When it's going down below.

Orange makes me feel warm and relaxed.

Tomek Pieczora (7)
Hillcrest Primary School

Orange

A red-hot sunset,
Fiery, hot sunset,
Flowers can be orange,
Like my flowers in the garden,
Flowers can be in patterns,
A bit like mine,
Orange is in stripes,
Like the tiger's stripes.

Cai Burton (7)
Hillcrest Primary School

My Orange Poem

Orange is the colour of leaves in the autumn.
Orange is my bright lunchbox,
It makes me feel warm.
Orange is my bright T-shirt
Orange is like the hot, fiery sun.

Jemima Harrison (7)
Hillcrest Primary School

The Stranger

The stranger sneaked slyly by,
His eyes like fire bolts in the wind,
His gnarled hands like trees branches.

He stalked down the steps like a panther,
His smile so beastly and bad.
He crept into the kitchen
I knew he had taken a knife.

Into the dining room he went
I followed him but was too late.
The blood was glistening on the door,
Dead bodies on the floor.

It was like a nightmare
I looked
He wasn't there
He had vanished.

Lois Cox (8)
Hillcrest Primary School

Untitled

An orange is squidgy
and orange juice is zingy.
Some cats' eyes are orange too,
I like cornflakes, they're orange too!

And an orange smells sour!
The skin feels rough.
Orange is the colour of the sunset.
You know the leaves when they fall down
Some of them are orange and brown!

Kira Rich (8)
Hillcrest Primary School

River

An oil slick,
A tail flick,
A flash of blue,
And orange too,
A moving reed,
A falling seed,
A sleek back,
A five-toed track,
A webbed foot,
A red-crested coot,
Polluted pool,
For man kills all.

Thousands of rivers die every year,
All plants in them die and no insects live
Under the rocks - because of pollution.
This is always our fault.
Old mine pipes rust and pour dirty water into rivers.
We have to save our world's rivers.

Alice Wilson McNeal (10)
Hillcrest Primary School

Christmas Morning

I jump out of bed in the morning and excitement fills the room.
I go to my stuffed stocking, and take all of the presents.
Very excited I tear open my presents.

There are tonnes of them.
When I get out of my house, I throw snowballs
And make a huge snowman.
But guess what . . .
. . . The day is over.

Clare Thompson (7)
Hillcrest Primary School

Shadow Strangers!

Strange shadows sneaking down the stair.
Floorboards creak as feet land on them.
He stands cautiously lurking in his lair,
The mysterious shadow stood where he was.

The shadow stranger came again this morning,
I don't know where he came from.
He sneaks into the dark backyard hiding himself from view.
The old oak he particularly likes to stand.
I heard his lonely cry calling.
Waiting for me in the deep dark land.

I wonder why he hangs around.
Just sitting around down there.
But now he has gone.
And I do not know where, but I know he will not come back.
He is gone.

Madeline Finch (8)
Hillcrest Primary School

Drawn With Shining Orange

You see the orange shining
On butterfly wings
Like shining orange paint
Splatted on a piece of paper.
The paint shines
Like the fire from the sun
Like a golden flower
That shines like an orange gem
And now you see the shining fantasies
Drawn with orange.

Polly Rorison (7)
Hillcrest Primary School

The Unknown Stranger

The unknown stranger gliding suspiciously
Through the dark hallway.
His cloak following him all the while.
The darkness creeps over him like a crawling spider.

He only appears at the dead of night
He floats down the stairs like a lifeless ghost.
Then the sun rose he fled from the wood like a leopard.
When I woke up there was a message on my bed.

Darkness fell, somebody floated in.
With a dark, sharp pin.
He was back
He floated in for a snack.
I heard him crawl all over the wall
This time I heard it all.
The dust rose from the floor,
He rushed out of the door.

Sophie Rippington (9)
Hillcrest Primary School

Magic Happiness

I am the ribbon of the Earth,
A mixture of both sun and rain,
Happiness of all fairies, elves and sprites,
All poetry, art and song,
I am the king of the stars,
The moon of all the planets,
Seven colours have I,
I sing my song, all day long,
Of course, I'm a rainbow!

Florrie Badley (8)
Hillcrest Primary School

The Thing

It emerged from the door,
With a petrifying stare.
It wasn't bald,
But had only one hair.

Its eyes were as dark,
As the black shark.

A thing called this morning,
It didn't leave its name or age,
Just an odd . . .
Strange, scary, spooky message,
And the dust flew away.

The next day like a flash of lightning
It returned and I was no more!

Frankie Pigott-Plowden (9)
Hillcrest Primary School

Great Snake

In a hole in the desert sand,
A snake lies asleep,
All of a sudden it feels vibration,
The snake awakes,
The snake uncoils uncomfortably,
And sticks its tongue out.
It senses a scorpion,
And slithers out of its den.
Fangs ready to kill
Snap!
The snake slithers smugly as it goes to its den.

Nikolei Joseph Suray (7)
Hillcrest Primary School

Battle Of Kyoto

It was winter, cold and white,
Twas winter when the emperor was executed,
And as his allies we were sent to destroy Kyoto.
We lost many of our samurais as the blankets of snow
And ice took them captive in the soil.

We were outnumbered ten to one but we kept on,
Invading all cities we passed, training more men.
The ice was what we survived on, turning it to water.

Then we struck, I was a unit in the trees waiting
To assassinate the king.
The snow and pines offered me camouflage
The hours went by and snow fell, so I waited.

As I crept out I saw crimson blood staining the snow-white ground.
I was the only one,
Even the king was dead,
And the snow kept falling.

Jack Boxall (10)
Hillcrest Primary School

The Stranger

The mystified stranger crept down the haunted stair,
He stared at me with a curious glare,
The parrot squawked like it had a bullet in its head.

The stranger looked upstairs and said,
'I'm going to sleep in your bed.'
He turned around and jumped up a stair,
He stared at me again,
Then he wasn't there.

Ali-Ahmed Malik (9)
Hillcrest Primary School

A Stranger Came To My House Today

A stranger came to my house today
It was a bit weird
He was very mysterious, he had a long beard like a bush
He stayed the night
But when the clock struck 12.00
We heard him downstairs making loud sounds.

Suddenly we ran downstairs
There he was all dressed in black.
He had a dagger, stabbed me in the back
Then everything went black
As I fell to the floor
He ran out the door
With me in a sack.

Ella Maggs (9)
Hillcrest Primary School

Strangers Running Free

I'm sure he was there,
Lying on the bed,
Trying on my hat,
That used to be on my head.

He bounced off my bed,
And bumped his head,
He went to the stairs ready to attack.

He has a white cat,
Her shadow pounced as she caught her prey.

So I have the proof of the stranger you see,
But no one will ever believe me.

Laura Ferguson (9)
Hillcrest Primary School

Tense Moments

And here she is
Writing at the front of the classroom
doing absolutely nothing.
Isn't that amazing?
She holds the felt tip there and then moves
it across the whiteboard.
Fantastic! What skill!
My word, she is in tremendous form.
But I do believe that she is having trouble.
Yes the pen stopped moving for a while then,
and I almost thought she was going to lose the thread.
But no, the problem was just temporary and she seems
to be in full flow once again.
The pen is moving faster and *faster*.

Finny Nugent (9)
Hillcrest Primary School

The Skeleton

The mysterious man walked down the road like a skeleton
He leapt in a limo with suspicious gloomy windows
He ran in my home with a deathly stare
And left a note in my *blood* . . .

A scary skeleton hand grasping for the door handle,
I could just see the note and it said 'Redrum' . . .
But I turned the mirror and it said, 'Murder' . . .

I could just see him running into the dark wood
In the distance.

Imogen Hawkins (8)
Hillcrest Primary School

Stranger

A ghostly shadow of a stranger
Floating down the stair.
His narrowing eyes
His mysterious nose sniffing at the air.

He creeps through the hallway,
Out the outside door,
Murders several people,
Innocents galore.

Suddenly he turns,
The sun was rising fast,
And it was time for him to go
He fled like a cheetah
To his crooked old house at last.

Ben Mason (8)
Hillcrest Primary School

The Hunted Stranger

A stranger went to hunt a house at midnight,
sharp like a silent louse.
He's quiet as a ladybird,
but wicked as a fox.
He had a dagger in his hand,
to kill animals and others.

The stranger slithered and hissed like a snake,
up and down the stairs.
But now he's dead,
in his bed,
no one even cares.

Syeda Zahra (8)
Hillcrest Primary School

Winter

Winter stole
Through the dark, cold forest,
Turning everything in her path,
To glinting silver,
Froze each animal
And everything else.

Winter pounced
On the chattering trees,
The trees lashed out
Scratching Winter's face.
Spring sprang out
With an almighty whack,
Killing Winter unexpectedly.

Matilda Everett (10)
Hillcrest Primary School

Strangers

So I'm sure he was there
On the top of the stair
All dressed in black
Ready to attack.

I was lying on my bed
With a hard, cold head
For I knew who he must've been . . .

So I'm sure he was there
On the top of the stair
All dressed in black
Ready to attack.

Hannah Wyatt (8)
Hillcrest Primary School

Strangers

On New Year's Eve, on a freezing winter's night
The moon was rising
The strangers crept on the street
A stranger crept into a large house
Carrying a large knife like a sword.

He tiptoed into a bedroom scared that he would give himself away
He saw a golden trophy, tall, taking his breath away.
He smashed the glass, grabbed it and ran like a cheetah.

Michael Sinclair (9)
Hillcrest Primary School

The Mysterious Person

It was pitch-black, the stars were twinkling brighter than ever.
Weird sounds were coming from downstairs.
Very faint sounds as silent as woodlice,
Croaking and creaking sounds coming up the stairs.

I tried to find a hiding place, hearing someone coming.
My heart was beating fast and my parents were scared to death.

Jacob Youngs (8)
Hillcrest Primary School

The Stranger

The hooded man crept into my house
like a black cautious cat.

He had a dark cloak with golden buttons
that shone like glittering stars.

In a flash like lightning he
disappeared . . .

Chris Whitty (8)
Hillcrest Primary School

Evacuee

I knew a boy who was an evacuee
He sat next to me, on the train,
His label with his name on read:
'Trembling Tom'.
Well it was certainly true
He didn't have a clue,
Where he was going.
He was shivering like it was an earthquake or two
I swear it's true.
He made me feel sorry for him,
The way he walked,
The way he talked,
He walked like he had a broken leg.
Maybe a wooden peg.
He had very tatty clothes and shoes.
Still very scared and worried of what was to come
He cried.
When the train stopped, he wiped his tears
And picked up his tatty suitcase
And left.

Ellen Sorohan (10)
Hillcrest Primary School

Upon The Door

I go down the stairs, I open the door
I see the snow
It drops and drops and drops
Like a feather gently falling on your head,
Like a building violently falling, falling, falling
To the ground until it starts to fade,
Melting, melting, melting, then the light is gone.

Edward Davis (9)
Hillcrest Primary School

Autumn Snow

As snow fell heavily like an avalanche,
The wind blew in silence like everyone is dead,
The snow shouted to the wind.

The wind blew louder,
The snow got heavier,
The roads were slippery like ice.

Just then snow, snowflakes came down like a lorry,
It defended against the wind and got into pain,
The snow fights against the snow.

The snow is hunting,
The snowflakes are hunting,
The snow are defeated, the snowflakes have won.

Everything has gone to the past,
We are in the future now,
Goodbye snow, we knew you well.

Gary Bell (10)
Hillcrest Primary School

The Ice King

As his icicle crown glows in the light
And his eyes of solid ice has its prey in sight,
While he waits his frozen breath gets faster and faster
His prey will soon understand the meaning of disaster
A torch of the snow goes onto his icy fingers
And he accidentally puts his leg in his stingers.
The prey sees the cape made out of polar bear's fur
And gallops away.

Maybe the *Ice King* will get his prey another day.

Patrick Carver (10)
Hillcrest Primary School

Winter

A cold winter day,
there was a freezing breeze
swirling and whirling
hither and dither
up down, round and round
as cold as ice,
as soft as a feather,
it floats through the air
like a leaf in a big winter breeze,
the cars are skidding and people are on snow-mobiles,
snowboards and skis
slicing through the ice,
the puddles had frozen up
and they were slippery and hard.

Ivo Perry (9)
Hillcrest Primary School

The Stranger!

One moonlit night,
In a dark, dingy dungeon,
I saw a shadow moving swiftly like a cat,
Suddenly a scream, as deafening as a hungry baby.

I clenched my coat and my legs shook like jelly,
My fingers unstuck from my fluffy coat,
I walked more and more,
I stepped in some green stuff,
It grabbed my foot and pulled me up . . .

Tara Anderson (8)
Hillcrest Primary School

The City Melody With Lights

The star studded night,
The yowling of a cat in the distance,
The howling of a dog in the far city ahead,
The gentle chirping of crickets in the dense grass,
The streaks of colour of cars, red and white lights,
This was composed by the night city orchestra.

The constant humming of cars drifting past my house,
The traffic lights acting as groovy disco lights,
The sudden shock you get when a skateboarder races past you,
The clump that is heard every day by everyone,
The voices of angry drivers getting lost in the swirling wind,
This was composed by the day city orchestra.

Samuel Gaunt (9)
Hillcrest Primary School

A Feeling Of Fear

The slum was his home but was like a sewer above the ground,
and when the war came, he was torn away from his home,
ripped away from the bare slum like he was some paper just being cut.
Getting on his train to the country with his suitcase full of hopes,
dreams and fears, but when he got to the countryside
his dreams all flushed away like a pebble in the sea.
His thoughts shattered like glass hitting the floor,
his hopes racing away like a dragster determined to win,
which left him with only his fears.

Sam Gurney (9)
Hillcrest Primary School

Food, Food Everywhere

Puma's pizza parlours
Sofa's soft sombreros,
Banjo's banana biscuits
and Paul's potatoes.
Finny's fantastic French fries.
I love Grandma's apple pies.
I go to Tesco and this is what I see,
French fudge from the fridge,
but that's a bit midge.
I go to the drinks aisle before I go
and see coffee cappuccino
This is what I see
on my shopping spree.

Jake Edmonds (9)
Hillcrest Primary School

Fear

Paralysed at the top of the staircase at night,
from the sound below it could be the deadly silence of night,
her hands drenched in her sour sobbing,
she was alone like a buoy in the sea bobbing.

What could be going on in the little girl's head,
probably thinking about her nice warm bed.

She is saying to herself *I can do it,*
I can make it, but it will never stop,
on and on like a bottomless pit.

Oliver Clarke (10)
Hillcrest Primary School

A Snowy Day

As the army of white men marched over the land,
It felt like I was in an occupied country,
The army of white were covering all the trees,
Stopping the sound from rustling leaves.

As I was stepping into the crystal snow topped with icing
The houses were frozen, the dirty places were no longer dirty.
All you could see in the ground were footprints
The snow was rolling off houses like an avalanche.

Haroon Ali (10)
Hillcrest Primary School

Snow

As the snow falls delicately to the ground,
The snow whispers like little ladybirds having a tea party,
Talking about little things.

As the snow fills up everywhere with titchy snowflakes,
The beautiful snow sparkles and glistens like silver pieces
                                                of glitter falling.

The snow's like pieces of Cadbury's Twirl winding through the snow.

Jo Nugent (9)
Hillcrest Primary School

Snow

The snow falls side to side with help from the wind.
The snow covers the whole of England with help from the wind.
My clouds shiver in pain with help from the wind.
The countryside swivels in amazement with help from the wind.
A person took me away into a warm house.
The curtains swivelled along the curtain rack with help from the wind.
I went to see my bedroom, for some reason everything was swaying
Around with help from the wind.

Amy Bolton (10)
Hillcrest Primary School

Fear Boy

Trudging along searching for a home
No house, no cave just left alone
His dreams shattered, his thoughts gone
He could hardly remember where he'd come from.

He clenched his fist and punched out his fear
As he shed a single tear.
He got so frightened
His stomach tightened with curdling fear.

He saw a light!
Flickering like shadows on a silent night.
As he got closer he heard no din
He tapped on the door and got welcomed in.

James Cockle (9)
Hillcrest Primary School

A New Beginning

A wondrous thing morning brought.
A beautiful feather of a swan
Or maybe it's a . . .

Plain piece of paper
Or maybe it's a . . .

Fresh sheet on your bed
Or maybe it's am . . .

Soft cloak of silk.

Whatever it is, it's a new beginning.

Conney Wells (10)
Hillcrest Primary School

Snow

Snow drifting through the misty air
floating gently towards the silky white floor,
covering everything it can get to,
its sparkling coat wrapped cosily round the Earth's surface.

The coldness of the coat is amazing,
it will lie completely still on the same land for days.
Otherwise creeping around freezing everything it touches,
choosing the best land to cover its favourite white coat in.

Sprinkling white dust over all the trees,
slicking ice to all water,
putting soft white cushions on top of every mountain,
and after his busy months he rests till winter - hibernating
through the summer.

Ellen Davies (9)
Hillcrest Primary School

The Time Machine

When I built my time machine my eyes filled up with pleasure,
I was really, really happy, and very, very keen.
I stepped inside my time machine to have a great surprise,
You'll never guess what I've seen, lots of massive -
Flashing lights and a big computer screen.
I couldn't see much else.
I heard a distant beep,
I came closer and closer
Until I fell asleep!

Raeanne Manning (9)
Hillcrest Primary School

Stranger Sounds

The faint soft sound of his foot on the stair,
was like someone bending a tree in half,
so eerie,
his breezy breath and haunted glare
had the same magic as when you plunge into a bubble bath.
His cloak was an oily black,
he quickens his pace to a canter,
a gallop,
until he is racing like a blizzard
with his foot in the stirrup
of a black horse.
His head in the shape of a haunted hook,
a black hood covering his lifeless face,
until . . . he disappears.
It came again this morning,
that dull lifeless ghoul,
disguised as a harmless shadow,
he's certainly no fool . . .

Amy Stevenson (8)
Hillcrest Primary School

The Crispy Morning

Fluffy, gentle, white, soft cotton wool
gently put down on a cake,
Like soft kisses from a polar bear,
Crystaly, icy and crumbly it falls onto the
top of the car and on the floor like a
blanket of snow.

Flakes fall down onto my hat and coat easy,
I am wrapped up warm, cold outside me,
But I'm not cold!

Jessica Bailey (10)
Hillcrest Primary School

Evacuee

Standing alone, staring weakly at the cobbled floor,
waiting for the train to carry me to safety,
the old battered train rolled in,
the fragile doors opened,
he hesitated, then walked in.

I arrived at the station, the wind was like long fingers
pulling my bags and hair away from the other evacuees.
I fell on my knees and started to sob like a poor person
on the streets.

Sean Byrne (10)
Hillcrest Primary School

Frightened

As I stepped nervously on the gloomy platform
The terrible screaming sound coming closer and closer.
Nearer and nearer.
I felt frozen like an ice cube cracking furiously.
I feel frightened not sure what my life will be like anymore.
As the officer came to take me away to my destination!

Sharratt Long (9)
Hillcrest Primary School

My Orange Poem

Orange is the colour of leaves in the autumn.
Orange is my bright lunch box, it makes me feel warm.
Orange is my favourite bright T-shirt.
Orange is like hot fiery sun.
Orange is how special I feel when I'm with a special person.
Orange is a piece of paper which makes me happy.

Nuha Najihah
Hillcrest Primary School

'Snow Joke

Running through the snow,
Nemesis breathing down his neck,
One more attempt to break the
'Hard-as-rock' snow barrier.

He knows what will happen if he fails,
Certain death.
He's through!
Knocking on the door madly.

There is no one home.

Liam Barter (9)
Hillcrest Primary School

Winter Wonders

The clouds fatten up to release flaky crystal snow
onto every living thing.
The army cloak cars and rocks forever
shouting into the heavens.
The ducks retreat from the vandalized pond
and fly southwards from it all.
The snow as frail as nothing ever before,
blankets the parks and rooftops of the white veiled towns.

Alec Coombes (9)
Hillcrest Primary School

Friends

F riends are true to you,
R ight behind you,
I n every kind of situation,
E specially when you're sad
N ever let you down,
D o things together,
S orry if they make you sad.

Nur Nabilah Zainudin (10)
Hillcrest Primary School

The Cold Snowy Night

The crystal-shaped snowflake,
Kisses your cheek as you walk along,
In the light soft snow,
Soft kisses from a big white polar bear,
As you ice skate
On the ice pitch.
When you go past the kids throwing snowballs
And kicking the snow,
The snow hits you as you walk along,
When the kids throw the snow all over you,
And all over the park,
As you walk.

Louisha Stanbridge (9)
Hillcrest Primary School

The Little Robin

The beautiful robin taps his harmless little feet on the ground
as the soft white snow drops like a feather floating
from the sky.

Still patting his little feet along the cold ground
looking for berries or left over food.

Next day still searching for food, he finds a bunch of fire berries,
but has to give them to youngsters back in the nest.

Always searching for him and his family,
there hasn't been enough for him for days,
so this might be the last time he has to search all winter.

Bethany Sordnan (10)
Hillcrest Primary School

Winter Week Poem

As soft as a feather
As icy as frost
As slippery as wet mud with a sparkle
As light as a berry
As crumbly as crumbs
As delicate as china
As white as paper
As clear as gold
As thin as air

What am I?
I'm winter.

Oliver Trace (9)
Hillcrest Primary School

Winter In Winter Wonderland

The snow glides dreamily across the world of sleep,
It continued the patterns on the white rooftops,
Blocking the way for struggling people.
The snow as white as falling doves,
Scattering all across the roads and streets,
Making nature's blanket.

The world is made into a white blanket,
As soft as feathers from your pillow,
Nature's crystals are being exposed to fluffy parts of cotton wool.
The world is now like a pillow!
The best place to rest my head.

Edward Ashby-Hayter (10)
Hillcrest Primary School

Snow

When the snow falls the rivers freeze.
When the snow falls you can find it
everywhere you go.
When the snow falls everything glitters
in the sunlight.
When the snow falls you can ski down it
and sledge down it.
When the snow comes it falls like parachutists
from the sky.
But the snow only falls once a year
and that's winter.

Archie Gunning (10)
Hillcrest Primary School

The White Snow

The snow is like pure white cotton wool
falling from the blue sky but with icicles
and sharp.

The cars are like big balls of snow
but some can move.

The small flaky snow all over the flats and houses
they all look like tall and beautiful piles
and piles of snow.

Snow on the fields look like you are in Iceland
with lots of snow instead of ice.

Elspeth Bond (10)
Hillcrest Primary School

The Curse!

The curse, he brought the curse
The man that lives next door
It's really bad it's really bad!
It travels through the floor.

It travels with that phantom man
That man with eyes of flame
He has a ghostly face
I know because he came.

I was scared
The moonlight was rising
My mum was scared
He was hypnotising
Then he was gone like the end of a nightmare.

Amy Baker (8)
Hillcrest Primary School

As The Snow Falls

The gentle snow slowly falls down from the sky,
As a girl looked out of the window,
The snow was blocking the way
So she could not see outside of her house.

The avalanche on the roof is struggling to get to the ground,
Its arms are as wild as a sabre-toothed tiger,
In a trap of avalanches.

The avalanche hits England,
We are doomed for life,
'We are history,' said a small boy,
With frozen boots like a cube of rock solid crystal balls.

Bradley Lewis (9)
Hillcrest Primary School

The Stranger

It was utter darkness
He rose from his tomb,
Unleashed his invincible shadow
And floated across the room.

He looked a terrible look,
A hypnotising glare,
A weird-looking face
He sat on his chair.

He looked like a nothing,
He looked disgustingly fierce,
Weird, weirder than anything
He started to sharply pierce.

He killed two sleeping children,
He poisoned four,
He darted through the room,
Leaving death galore.

He walked into the kitchen
Taking out a knife,
He sprinted like a raptor
Taking a life.

He left a freaky letter
He made it with his blade claw
Then he quickly, swiftly,
Vanished through the floor.

Then I read his letter
He had gone away,
Two minutes later
It was the beginning of the day.

Alexander Palmer (8)
Hillcrest Primary School

Spring Has Come

Trees put on a green fur coat.
Flowers erupt with an explosion of colour.
Fluffy lambs wake up and sniff at the pungent air.
Hedgehogs shuffle out of their winter hideaways.
The spider shakes the dew off his web - spring has come!

Reuben Leveson-Gower (10)
Hillcrest Primary School

Carelessness

Carelessness is a mixture, all colours
splattered and spilt.
Carelessness' smell has gone a little bit wrong
It tastes like a sweet with a bitter aftertaste
Carelessness sounds like things breaking needlessly
It feels like something that's slipped out
Of your hands before you have time to feel it.
Carelessness lives in little boys.

Lillie Grimshaw (9)
High Down Junior School

Life

Life is multicoloured
Life smells like a fresh meadow
with the acrid smell of cow manure
It tastes like whipped cream
with a tinge of rotten strawberries
It sounds like soft singing but
with the occasional shriek of pain
It feels warm but often there are
icy gusts of wind
Life lives in the soul
distribution section of Heaven.

Dillon Eastoe (9)
High Down Junior School

My Baby Sister

My sister is naughty sometimes
She bites my toys
Pulls my hair
Eats the sofa
Pushes the chairs
Shuts the door
Crawls round and round
Watches TV
Likes Mummy's keys
Wakes up at night
She has big brown eyes
Her hair is full of curls
When she has a bath
She smells so sweet
Then brushes her teeth
I love her and she loves me.

Joshua Walker (8)
Hotwells Primary School

Tiger

I have a thick coat of lava, what am I?
I have zebras' black stripes, what am I?
I have whiskers of a cat, what am I?
I have crystal green eyes, what am I?
I have the stealth of a leopard, what am I?
I have the beauty of a ruby and a sapphire, what am I?
I have the speed of the wind, what am I?
I have claws like blades, what am I?
I am as supple as a cat, what am I?
I am as wild as a lion, what am I?

      I am a tiger.

Cameron Byrne (8)
Hotwells Primary School

The Sea

The sea, oh how I love the sea, feeling the waves
between your feet, your feet getting covered in sand.
Oh there's no place like the sea.

You can make a sandcastle or two,
pretend to play prince and princess,
buying an ice cream and getting it on your nose.
Oh there's no place like the sea.

You can run and shout and play in the sand,
fly a kite or two.
Oh there's no place like the sea.

You can surf in the fresh salty sea,
splash and see how far the waves take you,
climb and explore on the rocks.
Oh there's no place like the sea.

Maeve Scally (8)
Hotwells Primary School

The Funny Poem

I saw a man flying through the air
with a squashed banana in his hair.
He always sat up in his bed
with a squashed banana on his ted.
I saw a lady in her underwear
who made the people stop and stare.
I saw a boy whose favourite joy
was flying all the way to Troy.
I saw a girl whose precious pearl
held all the secrets of the widest world.
I saw a baby who had no shakes
about her mother wearing skates.
All these things are really funny
and make our lives as sweet as honey.

Hattie Swingler (8)
Hotwells Primary School

Fairies

Fairies are very beautiful creatures,
They are probably known for their exquisite features.
Magical powers, gardens of flowers,
Shiny, smooth tresses, spider's silk dresses.

They live in a castle up high in the sky.
The clouds are made of puffy, pink candyfloss.
Fairies clean them with magic gloss.
Glowing wands change gloomy ponds into something fit
                                                                        for a queen.
The surface would now have a sparkling sheen
              And fairies are my favourite dream.

Evie Miles (8)
Hotwells Primary School

Don't Eat

Don't eat a welly because you'll be smelly.
Don't eat jelly because you'll get a big belly.
Don't drink rum because you'll turn into a plum.
Don't eat ants because you'll explode your pants!
Don't eat a dish because you'll turn into a fish.

Jo Thompson (8)
Hotwells Primary School

A Star

Every night a star glitters in the moonlight.
The little peaceful shiny star is bright all around the night.
Shining beautifully round the sky, glittering and gliding
                                                  through the night,
Leaving little stars everywhere.

Annys Whyatt (9)
Hotwells Primary School

Wicked Witches

Wicked, wicked, wicked witches
What horrible things they are,
Curses, warts and spells of course
They'll stir and stir until it's right
And give you such a fright.

Wicked, wicked, wicked witches
What horrible things they are,
Bat's blood and other yucky stuff,
They'll give you nightmares
Until you scream,
And you will get a shiver down your spine.

Wicked, wicked, wicked witches
What horrible things they are,
Broomsticks, hats and black cats of course
They'll fly away in the night,
To give you a terrible fright.

Hannah Marke-Crooke (9)
Hotwells Primary School

Henry VIII

One day Henry decided to give his servant his jobs
'Don't give me stale food or I'll be in a mood.
Don't let Mary lounge about or it will make me shout.
Don't laugh when I sneeze or I'll buckle your knees.
Plant me a rose or I'll chop off your nose.
Take me hunting baby bunting.
Catch those flea's or I'll snap those knees.
Behead Catherine Howard you sad old coward.'

Ailish Shallcross (8)
Hotwells Primary School

Zoom

Zoom, zoom, zoom
Running down the road
We're running to France very fast
Over the sea
Oui, oui, oui
Bonjour
Run to the market
Buy a chicken
Next stop the patisserie
Get some ice cream for our tea
Run to the beach fast as you can
Dive in the water
Run on the sand
Roll down the dunes
Back up again
Now we're surfing on the waves
Surf ashore
Make a castle
Dig a moat
Sail a boat
Now we're tired
Let's go home
Go to bed
Dormez bien.

Keir Byatt (8)
Hotwells Primary School

The Moon

Glistening away in the warm summer's night.
Moving away by the fat Milky Way.
Going under the black evening cloud.
Solid light up ahead.
Smashed plate on a witch's cat.
Shimmering away with my stars.

Harry Lloyd-Evans (8)
Hotwells Primary School

My Little Bunny

My little bunny
Sat on Mummy's tummy
With a jar full of honey
Then put on his dummy.
Whilst he was on Mummy's tummy,
He said, 'Yummy, yummy I like the honey.'
They were sat under a tree as the day was sunny,
Along came his friend named Ronnie Bunny.
'Would you like some honey?' said little Bunny
to his friend Ronnie
'No thanks,' said Ronnie, 'because honey gives
me a bad tummy.'
Then little bunny, his mummy and Ronnie all
laughed out loud as it was so funny.

Chirag Trivedi (8)
Hotwells Primary School

Food I Like

Food is fabulous, it is really nice
But it's the greens I don't like.
Fish and chips, chicken pie are the best
But it's the greens I don't like.

Sausages and pancakes taste yummy, yummy
Slop, slop going down your neck
Ketchup squidging out the bottle
But it's the greens I don't like.

Fishfingers are very fishy but they taste a treat
Mashed potato is lovely and tasty
But it's the greens I don't like . . .
(except peas I like those!)

Isaac Willis (8)
Hotwells Primary School

As . . .

As funny as a clown doing ballet in a cinema.
As funny as a president that's gone round the twist
With carrots up his nose.
As funny as David Beckham on Pop Idol singing the
Spanish National Anthem.

As angry as a sumo wrestler who's lost to a chicken.
As angry as the England football team that's been beaten by
Saudi Arabia.
As angry as a fish boiled alive.

As slim as a stick insect on a diet.
As slim as a pencil lead buried for millions of years.
As slim as a woodlouse folding itself into a ball.

As . . .

Fred Baker Turner (8)
Hotwells Primary School

Never Temper A Fairy

Never temper a fairy,
you'll turn out quite extraordinary.
If you don't eat your peas,
you will go sneeze, sneeze, sneeze.
And never have a fight,
you'll be in for a nasty night.
Whenever you leave your toys on the floor,
you'll hurt your hand and it will feel rather sore.
If you don't help your dad,
you will go very mad.

If you never want to turn out like any of these,
you will have to beg and say, *please, please, please!*

Fleur Baughen (9)
Hotwells Primary School

A Countryside Walk (Run)

Our dad took us on a walk one day,
We crossed through fields, mud and hay.
I said to Dad, 'Where are we now?'
He answered, 'We're crossing a field of cows.'
Unfortunately I was wearing red,
That was one of those days I should have stayed in bed.
But I went running at them 'shoo!'
That was the wrong thing to do.
Because they charged at me, '*Argh!*'
They chased me long and far.
Then the farmer told them off,
He told them off for showing off.
I asked Dad, 'Where are we now?'
He answered, 'Just another a field of cows' . . .

Bill Dunn (8)
Hotwells Primary School

My Baby Sister

Little fingers, small toes,
chubby cheeks and a button nose.

Curly hair and lashes long,
smooth lips, singing song.

A cute little smile and soft pink gums
It melts my heart when she holds my thumbs.

Kitten noises, tiny crystal tears,
A peachy bum and perfect ears.

So small and cuddly and very sweet,
from her beautiful face to her tiny feet.

    I love my baby sister!

Ngaio Danvers (9)
Hotwells Primary School

The Sea Waves

The sea waves like it's dancing to music,
It can't decide if it's going to be fast or slow.

The sea waves like it's trying to forget
All the bad things in its mind.

The sea waves like a move that never ends,
It's trying to remember how the beginning starts.

The sea waves like it's floating around
Until it gets dark.

Zoe Sherrell (9)
Hotwells Primary School

Animals

Cats
Cats it's a fact that they don't land on their heads
But land on their toes.
So why is it then, when my cat's by the fire,
His legs are in the air?

Turtles
Turtles, what about them?
You say they're slow, but I say they're fast
Because when turtles are born, they run to the sea
Isn't that right?

Bala Piti (9)
Hotwells Primary School

The Elephant Who Ate Grapes

Elephant malevolent had a hat in his pants.
Then the elephant ate an apple pie.
Elephant fantastic ate the grapes.
Then he had a tummy ache and elephant died.

Joe Lanham (8)
Hotwells Primary School

Summer

This is our summer place,
The trees are full of health and joy
Springing up very high.
All the leaves are big and bold
And the river trickles and tingles.
The air smells of lavender and daisy
Our voices are as sweet as sugar
And everything is bright.

Molly Jenkins (9)
North Road School

An Acrostic Poem

D iploducus have very long necks
I guanadons are small and very colourful
N ow they are extinct and disappeared for good
O ur land is now free, with no dinosaur to see
S and is now just on the beach with fossils as well
A nd now it's great with no dinosaurs invading
U nder pressure, no more of them here
R ound the world, not one dinosaur on the planet!

Rebecca Lock (9)
North Road School

Summer

This is our summer place
The trees are barky brown
All the leaves are glittery gold
And the river is cool and pretty.
The air is calm but breezy
Our voices are joyful and free
And everything is spectacular.

Zoe Potts (9)
North Road School

The Monster

What do monsters eat?
What do monsters eat?
Dogs' tails, cats' heads, guts of sheep
Pigs' eyes and rabbits' brains
That's what a monster eats!

Where do monsters live?
Where do monsters live?
In drain pipes, slimy and dirty,
Green, gruesome swimming pools
That's where monsters live!

What do monsters do?
What do monsters do?
Go around eating brains
Swallowing people's lungs and guts
That's what monsters do!

Sophie Bolton (9)
North Road School

Beth's Pets

In my bedroom I kept,
Ten polar bears drinking Coca-Cola
Nine koala bears hanging from the light
Eight beavers biting into a wardrobe
Seven black bears drinking lemon and honey
Six brown cats hissing and miaowing
Five baby fish swimming in the loo
Four blackbirds eating cheese and doughnuts
Three cows ringing their bells
Two monkeys eating bananas
One horse standing on two legs
And one *guess what*?

Beth Staley (9)
North Road School

Autumn Poem

In autumn it may look like it's hot
But it is not because of breeze there is a lot
Down off the trees the leaves will fall
'Look at the conkers!' the children will call.

The evergreens are still green
Against the tree trunk we will lean
All of the leaves are becoming dead
Up to bed you will need to head.

In autumn it will start to get cold
Different coloured leaves you will hold
It will now start to get darker at night
You will now need to turn on your light.

Leaves are rustling on the floor
Some people think autumn is a bore
But it is not just wait and see
It is a lot of fun for you and me.

Charlotte Causon (11)
Overndale School

Hallowe'en Poem

Zombies arrived from the dead
Blood is coming from people's heads
Bats are drinking people's blood
The graveyard is full of mud.

Witches fly in the sky
And they get really high.
Pumpkins are glowing
And leaves are blowing.

Benjamin Lynskey (7)
Overndale School

Christmas Poem

Santa is coming,
Santa is having a cheer,
People are humming,
Dad's drinking lots of beer.

Biscuits we will leave,
Up the chimney he will fly
In and out he will weave
The next year he'll reply.

Crackers go pop,
We love this time
People are shopping
I have a dime.

Francesca Causon (9)
Overndale School

Hallowe'en Poem

In October it's Hallowe'en
The scariest thing I have seen.
Vampires are appearing,
Dracula is cheering.

The witches are stirring
The cats are purring
The witch is flying on her broom
The other witches are in the room.

Katie Bennett (7)
Overndale School

Valentine's Haiku Poem

Doves are peaceful birds,
People kiss and people hug,
Cupid is lovely.

Flowers are pretty,
Valentine's, a time for love,
Sometimes people hug.

I have seen love bugs,
Watch here is a kiss for you,
People are in love.

Cupid might be near,
I love you my Valentine,
Valentine's are here.

Kerry-Dee Shaw (8)
Overndale School

Hallowe'en Poem

Graveyards late at night
Zombies come to fight
Gravestones come to life
The grim reaper has a scythe.

Skeletons made of bones
Beneath the graveyard stones
Skeletons make a rattling sound
In the graveyard they are found.

Jack Harris (7)
Overndale School

Autumn

Autumn is upon us
It comes in September
Stays for a few months
And leaves in December.

In England we call it autumn
In America they call it the fall
Who knows what they call it in other countries
We can only wonder, that's all.

The leaves will change their colours
To red, orange, yellow and brown
Apart from evergreens which don't change
And might not even fall down.

The conkers will soon come down
Ready to be found
Children will pick them up
But small ones will be left on the ground.

Georgina Daniell (10)
Overndale School

Hallowe'en Poem

In October it's Hallowe'en
The scariest thing you've ever seen
Mummies are in coffins sleeping
The frogs are leaping.

The bats are waking
The noise they're making
Witches are baking
The ghosts are taking.

Maddie Hopkinson-Buss (7)
Overndale School

Hallowe'en Poem

The Devil is red
He never goes to bed
Ghosts are white
It's a scary night.

It's a cold night,
The moon is so bright.
Wizards are weird,
They have long beards.

The pumpkin is weird,
It's growing a beard.
The witch has a black cat
She flies with the bat.

Megan Mulhall (9)
Overndale School

Christmas

Christmas is finally here
It's my favourite time of year
We put lights on the tree
For lunch we have turkey
Under the tree
Presents for you and me.

Father Christmas is in his sleigh
And Rudolph is showing him the way
Bells are ringing
People are singing
Santa is really fat
And he has a red and white hat.

Alexander Harvey (11)
Overndale School

Spring Poem

In spring blossom will grow on the trees
At the same time we will see the busy bees
When the sunshine is out
The bunnies are about.

The lawns need mowing
When the flowers are growing
The birds are singing
While the church bells are ringing.

Chicks hatch out from their eggs
And primroses grow out from the hedge
When we walk along the lanes
We see the lambs playing games.

Emma Ridley (10)
Overndale School

Christmas

Rudolph is pulling the sleigh,
As in my bed I lay.
Santa is flying in the sky,
Flying really high.

Crackers are banging,
On the Christmas tree baubles are hanging.
There are presents under the tree,
They are all for you and me.

Christmas is the best time of year,
It is finally here.
I can hear someone singing,
And church bells are ringing.

Rosie Pearson (11)
Overndale School

Hallowe'en

The vampire has sharp teeth
And on Hallowe'en he comes out his coffin beneath.
The mummy is out of his sarcophagus,
Now he is chasing after us.

The ghost is see-through white
And walks through walls and buildings all night
The ghoul walks through the night
Giving people a fright.

Declan Mulhall (11)
Overndale School

Rumplestiltskin

Weaving straw into gold is a very hard job,
The king wanted lots to make money, what a great big snob.
Rumplestiltskin pops up for a look,
Spins straw into gold but took,
The little girl's diamond necklace,
How people can be very reckless.
The king wants more lovely gold,
Rumplestiltskin comes back or so I've been told,
She has to swear to give her child,
To Rumplestiltskin mad and wild.
The little girl becomes the queen,
To those or so I've seen.
Rumplestiltskin pops up to see the girl covered in jewels,
'Hand over the baby, you're playing by my rules,
If you don't then find my name,
Remember now you're playing my game.'
She finds his name and puts a stop
To all of this, what a flop,
And so she lives happily ever after,
Her kingdom was filled with joy and laughter.

Sam Davies (10)
Rodford Primary School

Snow White

Snow White and her father lived happily,
In a great big world of fantasy,
Until he got remarried to a horrible woman,
And she fried him in the cooking pan.

The stepmother had a mirror that talked,
And she asked it questions as she walked.
But when it was at its wittiest,
It said Snow White was the prettiest.

She sent the huntsman to kill the girl,
When he saw her face it made his hair curl.
It was the most beautiful sight anyone would see,
He couldn't kill her, she had to be.

She ran to the nearest place to sleep,
When she went in she sat to weep,
Then some dwarves came back from the mines,
And said she could stay through her terrible times.

The queen heard of the news that she wasn't dead,
And ordered the huntsman to cut off his head,
She made a disguise with a poisonous apple,
And ran all the way straight past the chapel.

The dwarves found Snow White asleep the next morning,
They put her on view in a glass coffin,
The prince came by and kissed and carried,
The no-more asleep Snow White to get married.

Alice Phillips (10)
Rodford Primary School

My Pet Hamster Holly

My hamster's dead
And I'm sorry about that.

No longer can I see
Her claws scratch all the hay.
No longer can I see her sleep
All through the day.

My hamster's dead
And I'm sorry about that.

I cannot stroke her furry grey
And smooth back.
I cannot clean her cage out
While she has a nap.

My hamster's dead
And I'm sorry about that.

Now I can't see her eyes
Which were so very shiny.
Now I can't see her nose
Which twitched and was so very tiny.

My hamster's dead
And I'm sorry about that.

Lydia Lambert (10)
Rodford Primary School

A Kenning

A mad hopper
An insect catcher
A sticky jumper
A fly licker
A reed hider
A water lover
A green breaststroker
A musical croaker
A lofty bouncer.

Sian Pennant-Jones (8)
St Barnabas CE Primary School, Portishead

Stars - Tanka

Stars are very bright
The shooting stars are the best
Gliding through the sky
They are shining in the sky
They recycle light again.

Joanna Cox (9)
St Barnabas CE Primary School, Portishead

Dog

I watch carefully,
Not knowing a word they say,
I feel so left out,
But still I know they love me,
Because I'm a cute puppy.

Olivia Kincaid (10)
St Barnabas CE Primary School, Portishead

Skateboarding

I'm on a skateboard
I'm about to do a jump
I've just done the jump
I'm so cool on skateboards wow
Don't you just love my skills now.

Rory Atherton (10)
St Barnabas CE Primary School, Portishead

Bats - Tanka

Bats fly through the air
Biting and eating small rats
They are really black
Vampire bats cool but vicious
And they are my favourite.

Samuel James (10)
St Barnabas CE Primary School, Portishead

War - Tanka

The war has begun
People dying, people killed
The guns are shooting
Creating massive craters
The war has really begun.

Simon Shepherd (10)
St Barnabas CE Primary School, Portishead

Dancing!

I saved the last dance,
I always dance in the club.
I sing to myself,
And dance around my bedroom
Listening to my music.

Jess Smith (10)
St Barnabas CE Primary School, Portishead

Spain

Spain is a great place
The weather is so hot there
Really, really hot
You will need lots of suncream
And water will be needed.

Jack Rekesius (11) & William Ash (10)
St Barnabas CE Primary School, Portishead

The Eagle - Tanka

The eagle takes flight
Around and around he swoops
He circles the air
His wings whipping the air fast
Flying at amazing height.

Jenni Harding (10)
St Barnabas CE Primary School, Portishead

The Highwayman Poem

'When the trees creep slowly, hanging down the hill
The ghostly shadows sleep, sleep, sleep in the spooky dismal chill.

Where the horses sweat hurrying in the dusk
that started to gather

It is there that I will meet you
and beat you
Sir Traveller.'

Ameena Jassim (8)
St John's CE Primary School, Clifton

Highwayman's Wood

The owls hoot a mournful tune as they fly
You hear the piper *toot, toot, toot*, watch him pass by.
The trees stir strangely in the mist while he, the highwayman rides by
His steed alert, his arm a-quiver.

He sees the traveller riding by upon his noble mare
Your money or your life he thinks ruffling up his hair,
As the crack of dawn comes nearer
You see the blood that was once warm,
Now lying cold upon the corn.

With glee he gathered up the money
And looking as though he'd just swallowed honey
Rode off, delighted with himself
Knowing that he had won wealth.

Clare Hunter Funnell (8)
St John's CE Primary School, Clifton

The Highwayman

Where the gloom's walking to the sky of jewels
And the gloom is talking, talking, talking to the hills
And the highwayman is jumping with his black boots
The sword tightened, I was frightened
When the sword went through me
That was the end of my life.
'You Sir Traveller, when the trees were whispering . . . '
He took the sword out slowly, slowly, slowly and I
                                          fell to my death
The highwayman rode away very fast
And my horse ran away, away, away.

Adam Ebdy (8)
St John's CE Primary School, Clifton

Highwayman Hiding

Where the talking, desperate thistles wail,
Where the owl squawking, squawking, squawking
                                  calling for her male.
The spooky shadows limp through the whistling wind
                                  as they gather
'Tis there that I will stab you and grab you.

You Sir Traveller.

It is there the horses rear in fret,
And peer, peer, peer, when they met.
The animals blinded through the night, by the moonlight,
They shiver and huddle together.
I will soon threaten you, so don't be scared quite yet.

You Sir Traveller.

I am now so near you,
I will steer, steer, steer, I will scare you too.
Oh no, but he has . . .
Stabbed me right through
And I'm as weak as a soul,
I'll get you some day,

Sir Traveller.

Kate Brennan (9)
St John's CE Primary School, Clifton

Highwayman Poem

Where the terrifying frightening things sleep
You hear the shadows creep, creep, creep
In the dark night
Where the horses hurry down the gloomy valley in the mist
It is there that I will kill you by the hill
    You Sir Traveller.

Thea Rogers (8)
St John's CE Primary School, Clifton

Highwayman Poem

Where the wind howled loudly and slithered through the leaves
The gloomy shadows prowled, prowled, prowled,
                              behind the ghostly trees.
The twisty road wanders into the rocky hills becoming narrower
It is there by the hill I will kill
    You Sir Traveller.

The fierce winds cry as it fades into the pitch-black sky
The traveller's horse going by, by, by, as I get ready for him to die.
The dust under the horse's feet begins to gather,
I have already met you, someday I will get you
    You Sir Traveller.

Evleen Price (8)
St John's CE Primary School, Clifton

Highwayman Poem

When the fir trees cry and the wailing wind blows
You see a gloomy shadow spy, spy, spy with the dark crows.
You hear something trotting up the valley becoming narrower behind.
All that I can see in front of me is darkness.

Where the highwayman strides with his muscles all stiff.
With the spooky, dark owls all glide, glide, glide in the howling wind.
You look up to the sky above you
See the moon like a ghostly galleon.
The traveller sticks his sword through me,
My spirit rose from the deep.

Josie Brown (9)
St John's CE Primary School, Clifton

The Highwayman

My beloved bait, just you wait for my sword.
Just you wait, wait for you shall be no longer bored, never bored.
Where my gun blackened and my clothes tattered
It is there that you shall die.
'Tis there that your heart stops and your lungs will spurt blood.
    You Sir Traveller.

When all your riches paid and all strength begins to fail you
The rain begins to hail, hail, hail and your neighbours die of flu
Where the night falls dead and the children go to bed
You shall meet your death
Meet your death, death, death, for you shall have no more flesh.

Jack Whitby (9)
St John's CE Primary School, Clifton

The Haunted Highway

Where the dead bodies lie there I wait
and I dread, dread, dread, when you hear a spirit go to their fate.
The tree tilted, swaying in the gloom and fog that gathered.
All the ghosts creep out to play, then the head gets slayed.
    You Sir Traveller.

The wind slowly turns and travels the wild wood
And the fire burns, burns, burns where the traveller stood
And the rickety bridge swayed back and forth
And the distant mist gathered.
I hope to meet and greet you,
    You Sir Traveller.

Tessa Mathieson (8)
St John's CE Primary School, Clifton

The Highwayman's Night

You were travelling down to where I was hiding,
The animals were frowning, frowning, frowning while you were riding.
I was coming when you were frightened, frightened, frightened
to your death.
Twas you blindly searching for sight of me.
You, Sir Traveller.

I jumped out to where you fell to the ground where thy horse
was shivering.
I took my sword, twas above your head when you bravely took
out your own!
I jumped back when I saw and you'd suddenly jolted up from
where you lay,
You, Sir Traveller.

I jumped forward to where you were standing.
A clash of sword with the glint of silver.
I pulled myself up and it cut through your chest,
it was bleeding and blood dripped down
to where I was standing and the floor stained red.
You, Sir Traveller.

You then fell to the floor with a ghostly shiver.
I trotted off and left you bleeding and dying.
You traveller are brave but not as me.
And you were dead.
Sir Traveller.

Jake Thompson (9)
St John's CE Primary School, Clifton

The Highwayman

'Where the ghostly shadow lies
Where the ghostly gravestone stands
The highwayman will look
Shallow, shallow, shallow down on you
You Sir Traveller.'

Kaela Jones (9)
St John's CE Primary School, Clifton

The Highwayman

'Where the dark firs sleep and
the footsteps creep, creep, creep
along the crooked valley.

You hear the dark black shadows
Walk behind you, you, turn around
and the blood drips down.

'Twas there I will beat you and greet you,
You are scared and your bones have whitened.'

    'You Sir Traveller.'

Emily Perry (8)
St John's CE Primary School, Clifton

Highwayman Poem

'Where the wind howls mournfully and the trees shatter loudly
The white ghostly owl hoot, hoot, hoots through the leaves proudly
Where the horses rear and the stables open
It is there I will meet you and beat you
    You Sir Traveller.'

Danielle Lambert (8)
St John's CE Primary School, Clifton

My Sister

My sister's wonderful and sweet,
Full of cuddles for me to keep,
Lots of smiles for me and you
Sparkly blue eyes and soft brown hair
Tiny hands waving in the air.
She smells so sweet, good enough to eat.

Joe York (10)
St Mary's CE Primary School, Yate

The Gambler

Once there was a little man,
Who lived upon the hills,
He was a failed gambler,
His mind was full of bills.

But then things went downstream too fast
He had no money left to last.
Now he had no way to turn
So he called upon his friend to learn.

But soon his friend had lost his straws
And marched him straight out through the doors
He knew he had to run away
But where?
But how
And why today?

He clenched his fists
And bit his lip,
Pushing back the regret,
He was gone.

Hannen Ashlee (10)
St Mary's CE Primary School, Yate

Ice Age

It's cold and icy and freezing . . .
The temperature is dropping.
We're fading, fading away . . .
Will people remember us when we're gone?
We're running out of time . . .
Our heads are going down maybe for good . . .
We're running out of time . . .
It's now - twenty maybe more . . .
We're out of time
We're dying, dying
Dead?

Blake Skuse (10)
St Mary's CE Primary School, Yate

The Seasons

Snowdrops popping out of the ground,
Beautiful flowers grow all around,
No more signs of winter days
As the sun shines down its warming rays
It is spring.

At last the chilling days have gone,
And the summer heat has come.
Sunflowers growing higher and higher,
Whilst birds fly round the church's spire.
It is summer.

Leaves are swirling round and round,
As they slowly fall to the ground,
Squirrels collecting nuts and seeds,
Then scamper back up the towering trees.
It is autumn.

Ice is heavily concealing the town,
As the snow comes tumbling down,
Burying us right up to our knees,
It's certainly not the time for bees.
It is winter.

Abigail Woods (11)
St Mary's CE Primary School, Yate

Snow Falls

I wake up, what do I see . . . ?
Snow!
Quickly shove my clothes on
Rush downstairs to Mum
Can't wait to get outside
So out I go to make snow angels
And then a fat snowman
Mum comes out to see what I've begun
I just wish it would snow every day.

George Slade (10)
St Mary's CE Primary School, Yate

My Brother Lawrence

My brother Lawrence
He has a great name, I hope.
Every time I say goodbye
He gives me a great big kiss,
If I'm unhappy he talks to me
But I can't understand.
Well I can if he points.
He has brown hair,
Big eyes, their colour is blue.
He has a big smiley face
But as he's one and a half he is very annoying.
Well I did wish for him,
Because he's my brother.

Charlotte Northam (9)
St Mary's CE Primary School, Yate

My Cat Bobby

My cat has big green eyes
His fur is as soft as silk
His ears are bumpy and soft
Bobby's tail is long and black
Bobby has quite long legs
And his claws are as sharp as knives
His nose is wet and soggy
His whiskers are short and spiky
Bobby's teeth are shiny and tiny
And he runs as fast as a leopard
I love my cat so much.

Katie Pittaway (9)
St Mary's CE Primary School, Yate

It Wasn't Me

It wasn't me that broke the plate, it jumped onto the floor
It wasn't me, it was the wind
I didn't slam the door
It wasn't me, my hand just slipped
And curled up in a fist
He happened to be walking by
I happened not to miss
It wasn't me the knife just flew
Straight off the kitchen shelf!
It landed in my homework
I saw it do it myself
It wasn't me it's not my fault
Why do I get the blame?
The naughty child who does these things
Has pinched my face and name.

Robert McLeod (11)
St Mary's CE Primary School, Yate

The Lion

The lion's mane is really thick.
But the colour he cannot pick.
His teeth are sparkly white; you can see them in the night.
His tail has a tuft on it he doesn't wear it like a bonnet.
You have such large and fluffy paws they hide such ferocious claws.
As a hunter you are best because you eat up all the rest.

Jack Smoothy (10)
St Mary's CE Primary School, Yate

Across The Plains

Horses galloping across the plains,
Tossing their heads and shaking their manes,
Tails flickering showing pride,
Eyes are anxious, curious and wide.

Horses cantering across the plains,
Each becoming wetter as it rains,
Hooves flailing angrily on ground,
Each one conducting its separate sound.

Horses trotting across the plains,
From rolling each is covered in stains,
Ears tightly set back in stubbornness,
Each of these horses look a mess.

Horses walking across the plains,
Blood is boiling through their veins,
Scratching their hind-quarters as they walk,
In their own language, they talk.

Ashley White (11)
St Mary's CE Primary School, Yate

Friends

Friends are there when you're in trouble,
To cheer you up and make you feel double,
Friends are nice, friends are cool,
They make you want to stay in school,
No matter how big or small,
They are always on the ball.

Friends should be all forgiving,
Because they are always giving,
Friends are good, friends are great,
They should always be your mate.

Luke Sparrow (10)
St Mary's CE Primary School, Yate

Burning Fire

Fire is created from a tiny thing.
It can spread a long way too.
It can damage many things
Fire is like a slug it leaves a black
trail behind it, but not a slimy one.
Fires are vibrant colours.
These colours are golden-yellow, crimson-red
and burnished-orange.
Well that's what we think.
They're probably different instead.
Fires can be high, fires can be low
but highly dangerous too.
Fires can be hot
Fires are evil, like monsters and can kill.
Fire is all these things, so if you see one
keep away and stay away.
    Quick!

Bethany Rowsell (10)
St Mary's CE Primary School, Yate

Winter Love!

W inter love is a wonderful thing
 I n the snow when the snowflakes go *ping*
N o one out in the light of the moon
T he sun will come up very, very soon
E veryone sat in front of the fire
R eally warm and their best desire

L ooking at the snow still falling
O h listen, that's all the children calling!
V ery cold winter love but . . .
E veryone loves winter love.

Jessica Harrod (10)
St Mary's CE Primary School, Yate

Oh Dear

Oh dear, oh dear, oh dear,
Oh deary, deary me,
What's my mum going to say?
Oh deary, deary me.

I'm ever, ever so clumsy,
Oh deary, deary me,
My mother tells me so,
Oh deary, deary me.

Today I've stopped worrying,
All about my problems are over,
My problems are all over,
Oh deary, deary me.

Balloons on high,
Oh deary, deary me,
My teacher tells me that,
Oh deary, deary me.

I wake up, what do I see?
Oh deary, deary me,
It's an alien from outer space,
Oh deary, deary me.

Daniella Spring (9)
St Mary's CE Primary School, Yate

Secrets

I told my friend my secret,
I whispered it to her,
You promise you won't say it,
You promise you won't tell,
Because this is confidential,
I don't want anyone to know,
I can't tell you my secret,
Because it's *private!*

Emily Davies (10)
St Mary's CE Primary School, Yate

Why Is The Sky Blue?

Why is the grass green?
Why is an apple red?
Why is a banana yellow?
Why have the trees got leaves?
Why is the sky blue?
This is not true my child
The sky can be grey and black
Things are not always what they seem.

Alice Dudbridge (10)
St Mary's CE Primary School, Yate

Snow

Snow upon the houses,
Snow upon the ground,
People on the sidewalk
Or slipping all around.

Winds are whooshing through the streets
This I'll never forget,
Why do people love the snow,
It's something we never get!

Hannah Fry (10)
St Mary's CE Primary School, Yate

My Pet Mouse

My pet mouse Bubbles has fur as soft as silk,
And it's patched with blobs of brown fur.
Its whiskers are like a strand of hair,
And its eyes are like tiny black bullets.

Kerry Williams (9)
St Mary's CE Primary School, Yate

Taffy

I've got a hamster called Taffy,
She's the sweetest thing on earth,
She was one of nine babies,
When she hears a strange sound
She stops in her tracks,
All her brothers and sisters
Are dead apart from one
My sister owns him,
I have staring contests with her,
She mostly wins the game,
I let her run around in
My make-up box,
But she chews on my lipstick.
I miss her very much
When I go on holiday.
She's a bit chubby but still sweet,
I love her so much.

Katie Cardall (9)
St Mary's CE Primary School, Yate

Springtime

S pring is such a wonderful thing
P eople play and jump and sing
R abbits playing in the sun
I f you're inside you're missing the fun
N ever stay indoors when it's spring
G o on out and do something
T he spring memories are in my mind
I will never forget this nice springtime
M ild breezes in the sun
E veryone should be having fun.

Laura-Jo Stubbings (10)
St Mary's CE Primary School, Yate

My Rabbit

My rabbit called Bonnie,
Lived for three years,
Bonnie was plain grey,
I loved her so much,
I think she loved me.

She was so soft,
When I stroked her,
She rubbed her hand against my chest,
I felt so happy when she was there,
Another would not be the same!

Sadie Stenner (9)
St Mary's CE Primary School, Yate

Out Of My Car Window I Can See . . .

A field full of fluffy white sheep,
A yellow sun shining brightly,
Four great big railway arches,
A row of tall lamp posts,
A very bright enchanting castle,
A big, tall, orange crane,
Cars red, green, blue, white, gold and silver too.
All flashing by like a wink of an eye.

Katie Rogers (9)
St Mary's CE Primary School, Yate

My Cool Dad

My cool Dad he has a cool car.
It is really cool like him.
I look like him, but I am a girl.
No one is as cool as him,
In my eyes.

Olivia Flynn (9)
St Mary's CE Primary School, Yate

Sing A Song Of Football

Sing a song of football
Owen scored a goal
Beckham scored a corner
Heskey went mad
Germany lost 5-1
It was very sad
Then we had a shot at goal
But it hit the pole
After the match we won it all.

Alex Millichamp (9)
St Mary's CE Primary School, Yate

In My Brother's PE Bag

In my brother's PE bag you will find . . .
A pair of old baggy shoes,
Some ancient smelly socks,
A muddy shirt that doesn't fit him anymore,
A set of black shabby shorts,
Two daps that don't even fit my youngest brother,
Finally his jogging trousers all cosy and warm,
That is what you will find in my brother's PE bag.

Conner Foley (9)
St Mary's CE Primary School, Yate

From My House Window

From my house window
I can see . . .
Children playing on the grass
Lots of cars rushing past
People watching TV
Other people having tea
Then a man stared at me
It was only my dad.

Sam Martin (9)
St Mary's CE Primary School, Yate

Mum's Day In Bed!

Mum's in bed I said she should rest
Her head
A fish to wash the dishes,
A dragon to cook the dinner,
An electric eel to turn the telly on,
A bear to give us a cuddle,
A squirrel to put the bird house up,
A rabbit to tuck us up.
I bet my mum is happy,
Although I am not changing Katie's nappy!

Jessica Rudge (9)
St Mary's CE Primary School, Yate

From My Classroom Window

I felt very free and welcome when I looked out of my
                                    classroom window.
There were trees, hedges, houses and cars rushing by.
We are so lucky to have a place like this.
Benches, ponds, and windows, everything is perfect for you and me.
All I wanted to do was be free out there to feel the breeze.

Ellie Phillips (9)
St Mary's CE Primary School, Yate

My Cat Emmie

My cat Emmie is adorable
When she wants food she'll
Purr and crawl upon my lap
When she wants a cuddle
She will jump upon the sofa
And sit beside me
I love her so much!

Alice Rogers (9)
St Mary's CE Primary School, Yate

Once Upon A Rhyme

Once upon a rhyme
I didn't know the time,
If I had a date,
I would always be late.
I never fed the bat,
But I did care for the cat.
My mum made such a fuss
Over me missing the school bus.
After school I went to see my nan,
As I walked through the door she hit me with a pan.
I had a dog who tried to escape,
But it couldn't get past the front gate.
Once I went into a shop and nicked some sweets,
Because I couldn't afford my own treats.
I then had to do up my lace,
The next thing I know the cops are on my case.
I hate the cops,
But I love pork chops.
When I got home,
I ate a scone.

Lauren Wiltshire (11)
St Mary's CE Primary School, Yate

My Dog Buster

Buster my dog was . . .
Warm and loving.
Brown and white.
He was soft and looked after us.
He had a wet nose like a pond
And whiskers like ghosts
    But now he's not here.

Jodie Williams (9)
St Mary's CE Primary School, Yate

When I Look Out Of My Lounge Window

When I look out of my lounge window I can see . . .
Lots of cars rushing past,
Children playing on the grass,
People getting in their cars
Slamming doors very hard.
People watching television.
Then Mum comes and shuts the curtain
And says, 'Time for bed!'

Alex Martin (9)
St Mary's CE Primary School, Yate

Disgusting Things

'What is the most disgusting thing you've seen?'
Said Dean to Carl.
'A car crash, a dead cockroach,
Frog's insides, a fly in someone's eye,
A giant green potato, sick on the floor
Dripping everywhere,
Oh yes, one more thing . . .
You!

Carl Childs (9)
St Mary's CE Primary School, Yate

War Is . . .

War is one big row with tanks
That plough the battlefields.
War is muddy trenches with bullets
Being fired at the enemy.
War is people falling to the ground
And not getting up.

Jack Townsend (9)
St Mary's CE Primary School, Yate

Bear

The bear went down the street
Looking for something to eat.
The bear had some meat
From somebody's smelly feet.
The bear went down the street
He went into a shop
And bought some tasty pop.
He got a receipt
And went back to the street.
He saw a bin
And there was a tin and a pin.
The bear went to his house
Where it had a mouse.
His house was blue
And the bear had the flu
And that's the end of the bear.

Jamie Dadd (11)
St Mary's CE Primary School, Yate

Jumble Jungle

In the jungle all the animals words are jumbled,
They get puddle muddled with cuddled.
The lion has good fun but he gets that mixed up,
with a hot cross bun.
The monkey calls spinning swinging,
But at the time it was drizzling!
The snake calls slithering sizzling,
Obviously he wasn't thinking.
I told you they get everything jumbled,
I'm going home because I'm starting to mumble.

Misha Wiley (10)
St Mary's CE Primary School, Yate

Once Upon A Rhyme

Once upon a rhyme,
There's a loud ringing chime.
A man is near the dock,
And a girl in her frock.
There is a egg on the wall,
And a girl out at a ball.
There's a spider on my shoulder,
But the weather's getting colder.
I see a girl in the forest,
Though her mother's at the florist.
I sat on a pea
But I hit my knee.
Still a tasty gingerbread man,
Is running with a pan.
The last chime has passed,
So now I must dash!

Philippa Cutts (11)
St Mary's CE Primary School, Yate

Charlotte Moved Away

When my friend Charlotte moved away
I was very upset.
She had . . .
Long, blonde, straight hair like,
Silk that shines in the sun.
Two light blue eyes,
Small nose,
And a mouth that never stopped moving.
She had a sister called Emily.
They moved to America,
I wonder if she remembers me?

Alaina Herbert (9)
St Mary's CE Primary School, Yate

Once Upon A Rhyme

Once upon a rhyme,
There was a slug.
He started to eat some lime,
And a golden rug.
Somebody saw him,
Stamp, stamp, stamp.
The cat tried to claw him,
But the slug was too damp.
The slug saw the cat
And slid
Under the mat.
A man got a lid,
Whack, whack, whack!
He hit the slug,
And that was that.

Joe McKivitt (10)
St Mary's CE Primary School, Yate

My Brother

My brother can be trouble
and sometimes very silly
But usually he makes
me laugh, he can be very funny.
My brother can get angry
when I touch his toys.
He even runs away when
he's very annoyed
but he is a very sweet brother.

Cameron Kelly (10)
St Mary's CE Primary School, Yate

A Dream Of Sweets!

My mum shouted up to me, 'Time for bed.'
As I shaked and washed my head.
'OK Mum!' I shouted back, after all I needed a nap.
My head filled with lovely sweet dreams,
Of sweeties heading towards me in teams.
I wasn't scared because I knew they wouldn't hurt me,
And even if they did, I could just get something untasty.
Of course they didn't like savoury things,
Only yummy sweets and diamond rings.
But suddenly things just got scary,
Because I caught a glimpse of a beautiful fairy.
She told me I had only three wishes,
'Use them wisely not on rubbish.'
But ever so sudden, I heard a shout,
And woke up with a *fright!*

Katie Howell (10)
St Mary's CE Primary School, Yate

Food

Chicken, beef, carrots and peas,
They all taste really good,
Starters, main course and the pud,
Oh look it's time for tea.

Sweets, donuts, chocolate and crisps,
All for a midnight snack,
I should be having a nap,
Better food doesn't exist.

Very tired in the morning,
But I don't know why.
I'm eating and tying my tie,
Because it's time for school,
Oh how boring.

James Faulkner (11)
St Mary's CE Primary School, Yate

The Hamster!

The hamster,
The hamster, meagre and fuzzy
Nevertheless he's friendly and cuddly,
He creeps out in the night
Everyone's asleep,
The cage door's wide open
Out he crawls with no worry;
In my bed he crawls . . .
In my bed he crawls . . .
Until everyone wakes up!
I put him in his ball,
I cleaned out the coop,
There he was; safe and sound
In his enclosure,
Or is he?

Lewis White (10)
St Mary's CE Primary School, Yate

The World Of Nerves!

Everyone is nervous about the world of nerves,
No one wants to live there
The world is scary
The world is terrifying.
If you come here you're bound to leave straightaway,
So please believe me and do not stay in this World of Nerves,
Just run away.
When you get to the World of Nerves
You'll be full of petrifying nerves.
So please just go away.
Plus, if you go, most definitely you'll get nightmares every night,
Once again, please don't come to
The World of Nerves!

Jason Bradford (10)
St Mary's CE Primary School, Yate

The Spider In The Jungle

I'm in the jungle, it's a very weird place.
As I bend down to tie up my lace.
I look left and right, no fear I see.
I race on ahead but there's something near
I can't see.
I get thoughts of sudden death.
The paws and claws in my chest.
I see it run across the ground,
Look there it goes with my one pound.
Come back you cheeky devil and put down that
Silly pebble.
Argh! it's a spider!
Quick get me out of here.
I don't care how.
There's got to be some way out,
Or I'll start to shout.
I don't mean to be scary but I'm not good
With things that are hairy.

Alex Davies (11)
St Mary's CE Primary School, Yate

Limerick

There was a lady called Jean
Who was as thin as a bean
Although she was small
She was ace at football
And now she's the star of our team.

Jake Parsons (9)
St Mary's CE Primary School, Yate

The Zipodor

One day a father said to his son
'Beware of the Zipodor at Elmoflake
Fearsome and frightful to you my son.'

Through the fields the boy walked
Every step made him ache
And he could feel the beat of his heart.

In the cave it was dark
In his heart he was needing a lamp.
Slower and slower he began to walk
When in front of him he saw the mighty beast.
With big yellow eyes and a massive body
He had never seen such a bad thing.

The boy got his vipal blade
Left the dragon dead and slayed
The boy ran home triumphantly going, 'Yahoo yippee.'

Adam Fox (10)
St Mary's CE Primary School, Yate

The Lady From China

There once was a lady from China
Who wasn't a very good climber
She slipped on a rock
And tore a hole in her frock
And left her old skirt right behind her.

Bethan Ashlee (9)
St Mary's CE Primary School, Yate

Cats

Cats are cool,
They play with a ball.
When they fall they land on their feet.
Some people may think they are neat.
My big brown cat,
Sleeps in my hat.
She squashes it flat,
Because she is fat.
I shouted at her,
When she started to purr.
(Because she scratched the chair).
But now she has gone to a better place,
There will always be a little space.
I bought a new dog,
I nicknamed him Sog
Because he likes to play in the river.
When he gets out he starts to shiver.
Nathan Langley (10)
St Mary's CE Primary School, Yate

School

Maths is boring
Science is fun
When doing history you feel so young
In PSHE the world seems small
But geography makes it huge.
School dinners are lush; the roast to die for.
Literacy is kind of cool, when it's not the boring stuff.
PE is great, football's the best!
Art is horrid 'cause I can't draw.
School is good but an occasional bore.
Josh Gouge (11)
St Mary's CE Primary School, Yate

Racoon Rumble

Racoon, racoon, please stop fighting,
Racoon, racoon, don't be so frightening.
If you don't stop fighting you may get hurt,
And we'll have to take you to Doctor Bert.
If you come over here you'll be fine,
And your fur will be just divine.
You're going to lose against that fox,
So please hide in a deep box.

Racoon, racoon, you're making me sad,
Racoon, racoon, don't be bad.
Please, please, I'm begging now,
What was that giant *pow*
Oh no, racoon, I told you not,
And now you've gone and stupidly got,
A big black eye!
Looks like it's Doctor Bert for you and I!

Harley Thorne (10)
St Mary's CE Primary School, Yate

In My World

I never spend much more
than an hour
washing my hair in the shower
it always takes five hours
to make it straight so
why am I so sad all day?
'Cause you don't know me anyway
so what's the point in being right down here
In my world?

Sasha Tallis (10)
St Mary's CE Primary School, Yate

In My Bedroom

In my bedroom it's dark
I can't get to sleep
I hear noises
I am afraid.

In my bedroom it's dark
I can't get to sleep
I see shadows
I am scared.

In my bedroom it's dark
I can't get to sleep
I see things moving
I am frightened.

In my bedroom it's dark
I can't get to sleep
I hear screaming noises
I am petrified.

Katherine Powell (10)
St Mary's CE Primary School, Yate

Rugby

Up goes the roar!
Enter the teams
Dazzling white kit versus the blackness of night.
Handshakes, the coin tossed
Blow the whistle, start the clock
First kick, well caught, good run.
Tackle hard, pass the ball,
Again, again.
Knock forward declares the ref.
More ground gained,
Pass to the left, man in the clear.
Run, run, *yes!*
Touchdown, try, try, try!

Robert Bryden (10)
The Ridge Junior School

Colour Poem

Red is a beaming sun
The meat of a juicy heart
It sparkles with excitement.

Purple is an octopus dancing merrily
A plum sat waiting to be eaten
An umbrella bursting open in the rain.

Pink is the pale skin of a human
The snout on a fat pig
The smell of the scented carnations.

Blue is the sky at midday
The wavy ocean swimming to shore
The lovely bluebells sat posing.

Green is a spotty tree frog hopping happily
A leaf just fallen from a tree
The scent of green peppers.

Black is like a world full of stars
See them sparkle
In a world of darkness.

Hannah Dicks (11)
The Ridge Junior School

Pointless

A people killer,
A child hurter,
A weapon shooter,
A person scarer,
A kindness preventer,
A building destroyer,
A friendship breaker,
A people starver,
An unkind fighter.

    War.

Katie Wilkinson (11)
The Ridge Junior School

A Poem About Poets

Poets are very clever
I bet they write all day
How do they do it I wonder?
I must ask one someday.

Spike Milligan and Lawrence Binyon,
Michael Rosen and John Dryden,
Charles Causley wrote 'Mrs McPhee'
Jackie Kay about a hamster's holiday.

Another poet is Kit Wright
(And Allan Ahlberg seems to do all right)
J R R Tolkien wrote poems as well
(After the story of how Sauron fell).

Poets are very clever,
I can't write things like sonnets
But I've just written a poem
I've written a poem about poets.

Emily Kimbell (11)
The Ridge Junior School

In Simpson's Field

It was freezing, the man was wheezing
In Simpson's Field.
It was snowing, the woman was dozing
In Simpson's Field.
Hitler was singing, the bells were ringing
In Simpson's Field.
Churchill was shouting, the women were crying
In Simpson's Field.
The king was snooping, the queen wasn't looking
In Simpson's Field
The women were working, the men were fighting
In Simpson's Field
No one was in no-man's-land.

Bradley Parker (10)
The Ridge Junior School

Fantasy Poem

My dad thinks I'm lazy bones when I'm staring up into space,
But really I'm a devil
With my stick and paint on my face.

The land I often dream of is Spooky Land
Where you get sweets.
They're made from frogs and bats
And if you eat them you're dead meat.

Ghost and ghouls shriek nightly
They scare children in their beds
Buildings are made from sticks and bones
And everyone's underfed.

Oh, my dad may think I'm lazy
But what he doesn't know is
When the clock strikes midnight
To Spooky Land I go.

Jake Morris (9)
Two Mile Hill Junior School

Going Around The World

I am going around the world and I am going to take . . .

A gigantic, galloping, golfing goldfish,
A zinky, zonky, zappy zebra,
A horrendous, hippy, hoppy hippo,
A cheating, chattering, chatting cheetah,
A flying, floppy, flinky fish,
A tinkle ticklish tortoise,
A binky, bonky, bouncing buffalo,
An acid, acrobatic, angry antelope,
A loafing, lazy, laughing lion,
A jumping, juggling, jiggy jaguar
And me!

George Tucker (10)
Two Mile Hill Junior School

Going Around The World

I am going around the world and I am going to take . . .

An angry astronaut,
A special smelly stallion,
A crazy chestnut cab,
A monster motor mare,
A goaly golden gelden,
A fast footie football,
An icy Irish ice cream,
A wriggling waving water,
A running renalt rover
A dancing dripping dove,
An on off over,
A tricky tacky tack,
A foaming flying ferret,
A little light liver,
An eating enormous elephant,
A dirty dangerous dinosaur,
And me!
    PS I'll send you a postcard.

Nathen Scott (10)
Two Mile Hill Junior School

Going Around The World

I am going around the world and I am going to take . . .

An armoured avocado alligator,
A buzzing battery boring bat,
A crowned, cross-eyed, croaking cow,
A dirty, disgusting, doddling dog,
An enormous eating elephant,
A moaning mighty midget mouse
And me!

Ted Yates (9)
Two Mile Hill Junior School

Going Around The World

I am going around the world and I am going to take . . .

A creamy, clinking, clicking camera,
A tasty, toppling, tricky turkey,
A squeaky, sticky, silky snake,
A jumping, jolly, jealous jaguar,
A hip, happy, hunting hippo,
A flaffy, fat, fighting frog
A slip, slop sun,
A dirty, diddling, dart dog,
A kicking, killing, kind kangaroo,
And me!

Urlych Ingabire (9)
Two Mile Hill Junior School

Going Around The World

I am going around the world and I am going to take . . .

My disgraceful, dancing, dirty donkey,
A man-made mankey monkey
A lovely lemon lasting licking lolly,
My rave raging ratty rodent,
My chunky chocolate-coloured camera
A spitting, slimy, sloppy snake,
A cool, clapping, cotton cat,
A boxing, bored, bonker balloon,
A squashy, spotty squirrel
A wicked, wobbly, wonky, wacky witch,
And me!

James Wilmott (9)
Two Mile Hill Junior School

Going Around The World

If I was going around the world I would take . . .

A grey groovy granny,
A mad melon head mum,
A dancing and daring dad,
A prancing parky pappy,
A chuckling, chatting cousin,
A tight tricking teacher
An arty almighty auntie
An unlucky, unkind uncle,
A sunny smiling sister,
A bratty bad brother,
A shopping, smart Shannon,
A disco-ing diva Duffy,
A jumping jolly Josh,
A mouthy marshmallow Mathew,
A happy, hopeful Hannah,
A lucky, lying Luke,
A karaoke, kind Kayleigh,
An eggy elf Emma,
A splitting super Sammy,
And leave myself behind (peace and quiet).

Melissa Hooper (10)
Two Mile Hill Junior School

Going Around The World

I am going around the world and I am going to take . . .

My glittering, growing Granny,
My jumping, jammy joke box,
My magical, misty, make-up,
My daft, dark, dodding dog,
My lonely-looking lilo,
My sticky sand sweets,
My clever, creative, counting cat,
My swinging, sweet, singing sister
And me!

Demi Heaven (9)
Two Mile Hill Junior School

Going Around The World

I am going around the world and I am going to take . . .

A ridiculous, ratty, running rhino,
A bad, beautiful, big bum baboon,
A grumbling grey grasshopper,
A crippled copper camel,
A female petrified penguin,
My dangerous dumb dog,
A lazy, lousy, lying lion,
My brainy, bouncy, bright brother,
And me!

PS Plus a private jet to carry them all and me!

Josh Selway (10)
Two Mile Hill Junior School

Going Around The World

I am going around the world and I am going to take . . .

An aqua auto aunty,
A bulky brown bear,
A crashing, cunning cat,
A dirty, dribbling dog,
A eating eggy elephant,
A funny, fun frog,
A good gunning goat,
A hipping, hopping hippo,
An inky, interesting iguana,
A jacky joker,
And me!

Saqib Naeem (9)
Two Mile Hill Junior School

Going Around The World

I am going around the world and I am going to take . . .

A bouncy, batty, baggy badger,
An Egyptian, eggy, electronic elephant,
A cocky, creepy, creaky cockroach,
A zooming, zipping, zigzagging zebra,
A sticky, scummy, scribbly snake,
A powerful, pinching, praying pig,
A horrendous, hopping, hooping hippo,
A dirty, diseased, demonising dinosaur,
A clashing, classical, clamming carrot,
A manslaughtering, marching, manhunting mammal,
A lazy, lapping, looping lollipop,
A housewarming, hogging, holding hedgehog
And me!

Sam Price (9)
Two Mile Hill Junior School

Going Around The World

I am going around the world and I am going to take . . .

An aunty angry ant,
A bumpy black bat,
A crazy, cowardly cat,
An easy earthy elephant,
A fluffy, flying frog,
A good-looking giraffe
A handwriting, hard horse,
And me!

PS And a jet to carry them in.

Darren Godden (9)
Two Mile Hill Junior School

Fairies

My teacher thinks I'm lazy
When I stare at my pencil case
But really I'm a fairy
In a special place.

The land where I often go
Is full of lots of fun
The grass is blue, the sea is green
And the adventures just begun.

The sun is bright as Heaven
The sky is as dark as night
The river flows like cherryade
And houses lit by candlelight.

But my teacher still thinks I'm lazy
When my head's deep in a book
But really I'm sure she's jealous
Because she wants to take a look.

Jade Montagna-Malcolm (9)
Two Mile Hill Junior School

Going Around The World

I am going around the world and I am going to take . . .

My sunny, smiling, sparkling sunglasses,
My pounding pink puppy,
My ticking travelling TV,
Some cool, casual, clean, combat clothes,
My dangerous dancing disco dad,
My mongo-eating, moaning mum,
My brilliant, bouncy baby brother,
And me!

PS I will send you a postcard.

Joshua Grant (10)
Two Mile Hill Junior School

A Fantasy Poem

My father thinks I'm lazy
When I'm staring into space,
But really I'm a devil
With a really crazy face.

But down below you couldn't trace
It isn't half a deserted place!
The sky is red, the floor white
You would never ever feel alright.

The flaming lake is horn shaped
Poison ivy and devil snare surrounds
Trees leak white oil
Designed to make you slip on the ground.

Yes, my father thinks I'm lazy
When I'm staring into space
And although I'm a little devil
I miss my neat home place.

Mitchell Mainstone (9)
Two Mile Hill Junior School

Going Around The World

I am going around the world and I am going to take . . .

A sticky, sloppy, snuffling snake,
A bleeping, buzzy, bouncing bee,
A dark, dancing, dizzy dog,
A chubby, clicking, creamy camel,
A flapping, fabulous, fancy fish,
A massive, mighty, munching monkey,
A galloping, greedy, grey goat,
An arty, angry, agility, anxious ant,
A tiny, tickling, tango, twitching tiger,
And me!

Luke Price (9)
Two Mile Hill Junior School

Going Around The World

I am going around the world and I am going to take . . .

A slippery, slimy, slobbering, snoring snail,
An angry, acrobatic, annoyed alligator,
A bad, bad-tempered baboon,
A chomping, chumping, chimpy cat,
A dumb, dancing, dimbo Dad,
A miserable, mad, massive Mum,
A big bad breath smelling, bad-tempered brother,
A towering, tipping, topping tambourine,
A glamorous, golden, galloping, ginormous goldfish,
A tipping, tapping, tempered tank,
A snorting, slobbering, slipping sister
And me!

Brandon Curtis (10)
Two Mile Hill Junior School

My Teacher Thinks I'm Lazy

My teacher thinks I'm lazy
When I'm staring into space
But really I'm a little fairy
Not on Earth but a different place.

This place is full of wonder
Things not like we know
Everything was upside down
The centre place a rainbow.

Colours shine so brightly
Hues rich and true
And there's a deep pot of gold
It really is quite a view.

Sydney Barry (8)
Two Mile Hill Junior School

Dreams Come True Fantasy Poem

My father thinks I'm crazy
When I sit and stare at the sun
But really I'm a monster
With long spikes for protection.

In the land I visit
I'm the most powerful monster of all
The hot shiny sun chats with me
So does the chocolate waterfall.

The mountains in the clouds
Glitter and shine all day long
Trees and grass sing with the wind
But the flowers are too headstrong.

The river fizzes like soda pop
Buildings are built from candy
Creatures all have magical wings
Which always comes in handy.

Yes my father thinks I'm crazy
When I sit and think alone
But it is much more fun now
Than when I am full grown.

Nadim Ahmed (9)
Two Mile Hill Junior School

Going Around The World

I am going around the world and I am going to take . . .

A slimy, slithering, slim snake,
A bouncing, bopping, brown boat,
My chatting, chubby cousin,
My jumping, joking, jogging jeans,
A teeny, tattered teddy bear
And me!

Liam Wedmore (9)
Two Mile Hill Junior School

Going Around The World

I am going around the world and I am going to take . . .

A Billy Berty black bat,
A really, running rumpy rat,
A fragile, feely, fumpy frog,
An arty, arguing amphibian,
A clicky, croaky cat,
A little, lazy lamb,
A tight, terrifying tiger,
A grumpy, groaning giraffe,
A humpy, hungry, hairy hippo,
A poorly, panicking pony,
An early, energetic elephant,
A zippy, zzzzzping zebra,
And me!

Lucy Lintern (9)
Two Mile Hill Junior School

Going Around The World

I am going around the world and I'm going to take . . .

An aggravating, annoying artichoke,
A boring banana bungle,
A catapulting, careless caterpillar,
A dirty, ducking dog,
An eggy egg ET,
A funky, floppy fudge,
A glad, galloping guitar,
A hoppng, happy hippo
And me!

Mitchell Tuff (9)
Two Mile Hill Junior School

When I'm Older

I always thought I'd like to be famous,
I wasn't really sure what though.

I could be an astronaut and float all over space,
Or a drummer drumming on bass,
I could be an actor and star in the best films.

Maybe a singer and win loads of competitions,
Maybe even sail around the world like Christopher Columbus
Or discover a new disease.

I always thought I'd like to help people,
By donating money,
Or making a cure for cancer,
I could be a vet and give treatment,
Or maybe a nurse and give serious operations.

It just goes to show,
That there are thousands of opportunities and things to do,
But after all of my thoughts I'd rather be
    Me!

Abbie Fish (10)
Two Mile Hill Junior School

Going Around The World

I am going around the world and I am going to take . . .

My beautiful, big, baby-blue bag,
My magical, massive, marvellous money,
My snazzy, snappy, super sunglasses,
My casual, catchy, calamity clothes,
My glimmering, glorious, glittering gymnastic,
My jazzy, jumping, jangling jewellery,
My mystical, magical make-up mirror
And me!

Shannon Davies (10)
Two Mile Hill Junior School

Going Around The World

I am going around the world and I am going to take . . .

A bouncing, bing-bong bucket,
Smiley, shining sunglasses,
Wavy wishing water,
A hanging, hairy hairbrush,
A bright, brilliant bandanna,
A damaged, dangerous donkey,
A brown broken boat,
My tall, tidy teddy,
My magical, moonlight make-up,
A clever clicking camera,
And me!

Elleney Threader (10)
Two Mile Hill Junior School

Going Around The World

I am going around the world and I am going to take . . .

One ziggy, zappy, zippy Zimbabwe zip,
A morning, moaning, miserable, mapping mat,
An annoying, acrobatic, awesome armchair,
A sizzling, sly, smiley, sarcastic sofa,
A flying, flapping, funny fridge,
A happy, hard, heavy hat,
A nasty, naughty napkin,
A ticking, tocking, terrific towel,
And me!

PS Everything but the kitchen sink (actually I am taking it).

Zoe Burchill (10)
Two Mile Hill Junior School

Football Trouble

Football managers are never pleased
Big and fat and always getting teased
Sending orders to tackle and run
But while running he weighs a ton.
As he sits in a pub
He's gonna send us to another club
We all know what happened to Beckham
So when we get a manager we better check him.
As we all get sent away
We all secretly run and play
As we play for a brand new team
The crowd gets ready to jump and scream.
Everyone is really proud
Taking their shirt off in front of the crowd.
If the crowd gets all uptight
Then both of the teams will get in a fight.
If we didn't do what the manager said
We will end up with a boot in the head.
All the players get really mad
When the manager thinks we're bad.
Everyone treats us just like dirt
Just because of our yellow coloured shirt.
It's not our fault about the kit
Even if we do look like a clown in it.
The people that hate football are usually posh,
When all we're doing is getting some extra dosh.
Now our stadium has been burnt
I think we have our lesson learnt.

Charley Millard (11)
Two Mile Hill Junior School

Football

Ball kicker
Knee hurter
Ball dribbler
Ball handler
Free kicker
Goal scorer
Ball spanner
Penalty kicker
Goal kicker
Face seater
Ball tackler
Red card giver
Goal hanger
Goal celebrator
Man of the match.

Joab Magara
Two Mile Hill Junior School

Going Around The World

I am going around the world and I am going to take . . .

A clicking, clanking camera,
My dangerous, deadly dagger,
My murderous mother,
A sandy scorpion,
A pecking, punching pencil,
My joking junior joke book,
My silly, shy, slushy sister,
A rotten rat,
A painful puzzle,
A snappy shark,
A dangerous, deadly dragon,
And me!

Bradley Raynard (9)
Two Mile Hill Junior School

Chinese New Year

On the twelfth day of New Year I came to like . . .

> Twelve funny monkeys
> Eleven purring tigers
> Ten fire dragons
> Nine munching snakes
> Eight raging oxen
> Seven eating roosters
> Six talking sheep
> Five galloping horses
> Four barking dogs
> Three raging rats
> Two jumping rabbits
> And a pig in a tea tray.

Ellis Fitzgerald (10)
Two Mile Hill Junior School

The Witch Next Door

There was a grumpy witch next door
She thought she had lots of money, she was poor
She had a brand new black cat
After that she turned it into a bat
The old grumpy witch collected slugs
Before the witch knew it all of them turned into mugs.

She didn't have any sense
Only to put up a fence
So she could have some time alone
To have sometime on the phone
That was about the witch's life
She ended it all with a knife.

Samantha Pomroy (11)
Two Mile Hill Junior School

Family And Friends!

F is for fun that's what we have
A is for always being there
M is for making me madly happy
I is for the intelligence you gave me
L is for loving me like I love you
Y is for you, you care, you know.

A is for action, abseiling we've done
N is for noseing in my room
D is for dancing around the dance floor.

F is for our fantastic friendship
R is for your radiant smile
I is for ice cream we share at the park
E is for entertainment that's what you bring
N is for your nursing hands
D is for daydreaming about the good times
S is for saying let's go . . . *shopping*

    You will always be in my heart!

Rhiannon Bennett (10)
Two Mile Hill Junior School

Can You?

Can you eat coconuts off the palm of your hand?
Can you bang the drum in your ear like a pop band?
Can your hair hop as quick as it can
Or does it have to take time . . .
Like my friend Dan?

Can you use sign language for my sis Mat?
Can you pull out a rabbit from a top hat?
Can your pet dog make patterns like a pattern on a mat
Or does it have to take time . . .
Like my friend Pat?

Sania Ali (10)
Two Mile Hill Junior School

What Do I Believe?

Do I believe the sun is yellow?
No I believe it is red.
Do I believe the sky is mellow?
Yes it's soft like bread.
Do I believe the moon is bright?
Yes dullness has never been found.
Do I believe day is night?
No I believe it's the other way round.
Do I believe I was a monkey?
No I believe I was an ape.
Do I believe disco lights are funky?
No they are as dull as a grape.
Do I believe in the creation story?
Yes some of it was true.
Do I like the name Dori?
Yes it's a name for you.
Do I believe? Do I believe?
What do I believe?
Well one day I will know.

Eilidh Elder (11)
Two Mile Hill Junior School

It Goes Pop

Coca-Cola come into town
Diet Pepsi shot them down
Dr Pepper picks them up
And now they've all got 7-Up
Superman flying there in his jazzy underwear
Looking for his Lois Lane
Is it a bird or is it a plane?

George Mattock (10)
Two Mile Hill Junior School

Football Trouble

Football can hurt in all different places
If you don't tie up your laces
Get sent off, get a warning
You know you'll regret it in the morning.

Yell at the ref all you like
After tell him to take a hike
When the ball ends in the back of the net
The goalie brings up a terrible sweat.

The other team shoot to bring a goal
But the goalie saves it using all his soul
The referee took a free kick
But he kicked it as hard as a brick.

The player walks up to the line to shoot
He kicks it hard with his boot
The crowd watched in a daze
And when he scored they went into a craze.

The whistle blows for the end of the match
And the players have left the pitch leaving a muddy patch
The ref has given out one red card
And that player was in the dog's yard!

Tom Willett (11)
Two Mile Hill Junior School

Claustrophobia

I *hate* being in cramped spaces.
Like water is afraid of being put in a glass.
Like a pencil is afraid of being shut in a pencil case.
Like money is afraid of being pushed into a till.
Like a book is afraid of having its pages ripped out.
Like a TV is afraid of being turned on and off.
Like a ruler is afraid of being snapped.
Like a dish is afraid of the cloth and water.

I hate being in cramped spaces!

Emmy Willett (11)
Two Mile Hill Junior School

My Dog!

My dog is black and white
She loves to sleep day and night
My dog is always friendly
She goes after food at night.

My dog is black and white
She loves little people like girls
My dog barks at the door every morning
She likes going out for a walk every morning.

My dog is black and white
She lies going out finding logs
My dog licks you on your face
She eats lots of food like dog food.

My dog is black and white
She likes playing with a kite
My dog sleeps on a table or a chair
My dog is black and white.

Jacqueline Stokes (11)
Two Mile Hill Junior School

Going Around The World

I am going around the world and I am going to take . . .

A thick, tedious, tender teacher,
An obvious, offensive, outrageous ogre,
A keen, knowing, kind kingfisher,
A young, yellow, yoghurty yak,
An okay, obedient, obnoxious, oily ox,
A rightful, rickety, riddling rhino,
An ugly, ungrateful, unsteady unicorn,
A laughing, lush, loopy lion,
An eating, excellent, exciting eagle,
A soaring, successful, snappy seagull
And me!

Hannah Smale (10)
Two Mile Hill Junior School

Moon Dance

I've got a pet dolphin
Her best friend is a whale.
She dances fast and slow
Splashing her tail.

Up and down
She dances in the moonlight.
All day and night,
In the bright light.

She catches her food
Like small fish,
But on the other hand
She's very ticklish.

I love her so much
She's cuddly and cute.
She comes when I play
The magic flute.

Hannah Gunningham (8)
Two Mile Hill Junior School

The Sea

The sea is like a big bed.
The sea is thunder.
The sea is like a calm river.
The sea is a big blue dolphin.

Nicholas Owen (10)
Two Mile Hill Junior School

Football Matches

Football matches are cool and thrilling
They also keep people chilling
It's eleven a side
Plus the goal nets are very wide
Two different teams
Come and break their spleens.

Football managers are never pleased
Big, fat and always get teased
They sit in a pub
They're thinking about sending us to a different club
They shout and scream
As they plan another scheme.

The match starts, the whistle blows
The two teams have different clothes
The ball gets carried from leg to leg
When the goal is in the keeper begs.

A penalty is given
The ball gets power driven
The back of the net it goes
The keeper sees it up-close.

The ref gives a red card warning
That will hurt in the morning.
The other team finally scores
And all around a sudden roar
They bring on a sub
He sits in a tub
The ref took a free kick
He kicked as hard as you lob a brick.

The end of the match appears
The cheerleaders starts to cheer.

Jake Haskins (11)
Two Mile Hill Junior School

History!

First there was the big bang
Some believe God was the man
Atoms formed to create the world
Dinosaurs evolved rolled up curled.

Tutankhamen lived in a tomb until Carter came and disturbed him
He went back to bed and knocked off his head
So Carter didn't go back to find him.

Then came the Romans
Caesar was a low man
He went on a ship
And invaded the Brits.

Then came the Tudors 1485 'til 1603
Henry VIII was his name
The fattest king to ever reign
He had six wives and they all died
So that was the end of his game.

Next came the Victorians
She, the Queen ruled them
Her husband got killed
She had smallpox and dealed.

Then came the Blitz
With all those horrible nits
They had . . .
Guns to shoot
Weapons to use
And bombs to destroy the terrible fight.

So that was that all 'n' all
History
Playing its game!

Laura Bloomfield (11)
Two Mile Hill Junior School

Claustrophobia

I am scared of the dark
Like a pen/pencil is afraid of a piece of paper,
Like a piece of bread is afraid of butter,
Like a CD is afraid of a CD player,
Like a bookshelf is afraid of a book,
Like a rubber is afraid of a pencil,
Like a shoe is afraid of a foot,
Like a video is afraid of a video player,
Like a wall is afraid of wallpaper,
Like a cat is afraid of a dog,
Like an elephant is afraid of a mouse!

What are you afraid of
And what is the same as that or what is, as similar as that?

Jessica Maggs (10)
Two Mile Hill Junior School

My Granny's Dog

My granny has a lovely dog
And Dudley is his name
He sometimes does as he's told
Which can be quite a pain
When we take him on the beach
Swimming is his game
He'll swim the length of the beach
There and back again
But then when he's tired
He'll fall asleep
And be good as gold
It's about the only time
He'll be real good
And do just as he's told.

Grace Reed (10)
Two Mile Hill Junior School

My Future Job

I'd like to be a police officer and say, 'You're *nicked!*'
I'd like to be an archaeologist and say, 'Amazing find,'
I'd love to be a zookeeper and say, 'Clean up that mess!'
There's just so many jobs I really can't make up my mind!

I'd love to be a pop star and sing with Britney Spears.
I'd love to be a model and stride down the aisle.
I'd love to be an actress like Marilyn Monroe,
Hey somebody pass me the phone here, I really need to dial!

I'd love to be a solicitor and be way in control,
I'd love to be a vet and help animals in danger,
I'd love to be a nurse and find the cure for cancer,
Oh my God, all these jobs, somebody pass me my pager!

But most of this doesn't compare to the one job I really want
It's good, it's fun and everything they're not.
I'd like to be a nice person,
And be a real bright light on the world.

Poppy Hynam (10)
Two Mile Hill Junior School

Going Around The World

I am going around the world and I am going to take . . .

A jumping, junior, joking jackal,
A mad, murderous, massive Mother,
A dopey, dangerous, drooling dog,
A faking, forgetful Father,
A slippery, slimy, snapping sister,
A badly behaved brother,
A puffing, panting, pounding pony,
A clicking, clapping, clockwork camera,
A hopping, hissing horse,
A licking, lapping, lonely lion.
And me!

Michael Lock (10)
Two Mile Hill Junior School

Snow White And The Seven Dwarves

One cold winter's night,
The queen was praying with all her might,
For a loving little child,
With black hair so tender and mild.

One day her willing wish came true,
She was was so surprised she didn't have a clue,
But one very sad day,
The queen slowly passed away.

The king decided to marry again,
To an evil witch that had used lots of men,
One day she said to the mirror on the wall,
'Who is the fairest of them all?'

Unfortunately he said Snow White,
The witch stepped back in a terrible fright,
She sent Snow White with a guard to the wood,
She begged not to kill her and he understood.

Chelsie Bridgeman & Lauren Barnes (10)
Two Mile Hill Junior School

The Little Match Girl

A little girl was left alone
With nowhere warm to call her home.

Out on the street to sell her wares,
All alone nobody cares.

People pass her no one buys them,
Can't go back until she sells some.

She lights her matches to keep warm
Gran arrives in her ghostly form.

Taken her soul but left her there
Now dead everyone stops to stare.

Karla Dowding (10)
Two Mile Hill Junior School

Going Around The World

I am going around the world and I am going to take . . .

My manky, mangy, minging mobile,
My sunny, silly, shining sunglasses,
My tickly, tangy, Tilly the teddy,
My dingy, disturbing, dirty dog,
My green glass, grassy globe,
My boxing, boxy, boring boxer,
My flippy, flushing, florescent fish,
My rugged, rough rubber ring,
My mousy, mouldy money,
My angry, able aunty,
My tiny, tired TV,
And me!

Samantha Gould (10)
Two Mile Hill Junior School

Insects

Insects are cool
Insects are great
They would wriggle
And wriggle if you
Put them on a plate.
I wouldn't like ants
Sat in my pants
But I would like to
Wriggle all the way to
France.
The ladybird
The ladybird flew away
Not because of the fire
Because she wanted
To play.

Monique Ash (8)
Two Mile Hill Junior School

Going Around The World

I am going around the world and I am going to take . . .

My moaning mingy monkey,
My fat funny frog,
My dinky doodle donkey,
My clonky clock crab,
My dancing diddle dolphin,
My great good giraffe
My oozing old owl,
My anti-antic ant,
My sweet sherbet sweets,
My favourite fast flowers,
My catching cool cat,
My beautiful baby brother,
My marvellous mummy,
My daring dad,
My cute, cool car,
My large laughing mansion,
My sunny suntan stuff,
My fab, fierce fairy,
My cool clown,
My rough, running rabbit,
My fabulous friend,
My booming backward boomerang,
My doodle dancing dog,
My room size radio,
My delightful, dearest Darren,
My lovely likeable Lewis,
My fabulous funky family
And me!

Lauren Preece (9)
Two Mile Hill Junior School

The Lane Of Fire And Ice

The lane I walked down every day
The lane which caused my death
The lane which caused my suffering
The lane of fire and ice
Gone now from this world I am
Long departed, forever, forgotten
My soul has been torn asunder
My friends have all left me
I should never have taken the trip
Down the lane of fire and ice
How long have I been here I do not know
Everyday seems like a year
In this chamber I will dwell
In the lane of fire and ice
I am just a spirit now
A shining snow-like mist
The ghost of a boy
Who took an early death
Down the lane of fire and ice
I cannot leave this lane
Bound for all eternity
Locked in the lane I entered once
The lane of fire and ice
But if a foolish person would enter
The lane of fire and ice
I would claim his life
Because I died here
And whoever enters
Will die too
In the lane of fire and ice.

Daniel Cantle (11)
Two Mile Hill Junior School

Going Around The World!

I am going around the world and I am going to take . . .

A freezing frosty fridge,
A squirty soft suncream,
Some sunny shiny sunglasses,
A big bouncy beachball,
A warm woolly jumper,
A tiny tatty towel,
And me!

Kayleigh Evans (10)
Two Mile Hill Junior School

Home From School

Home from school seeing Mum spraying her perfume,
Seeing Dad on the computer working madly
Fish looking at fish food.

Seeing animals in the field eating grass,
Dogs waking smartly and calmly.
Mum's arms ready to give me a huge hug,
Seeing patterns on wallpaper.

Tasting solid hard sweets curling on my mouth,
Tasting the crunchy biscuit crumbs going on the floor,
Nuttella sandwich ready to be eaten
The cold fresh water lovely and silky blue.

Smelling the chicken pie just roasting,
Smelling the cat fur from picking up cats,
Smelling fish food for hungry fish.

Touching the smooth sofa ready to watch
Feeling the TV buttons pressing which one.

Hearing the kettle boiling,
Hearing the floor being scuffled by shoes
Hearing music played in another room
Hearing the birds singing peacefully in the garden.

Megan Fowler (9)
Ubley Primary School

Home From School

Seeing a massive long smooth banister
Seeing George sprinting to the TV
Seeing the dark rough carpet.

Hearing George stamping incredibly
Hearing a sharp knife cutting loudly
Hearing an old TV screaming.

Touching a pair of old TV controls
Touching a big apple
Touching a new green mug.

Tasting milky hot chocolate
Tasting a crunchy apple
Tasting curry in my mouth.

Smelling delicious food in the pan
Smelling cocoa as it goes into my mouth
Smelling toast as it goes into my mouth.

Charles Mitchell (8)
Ubley Primary School

Home From School

I can see a massive bookshelf with all sorts of books
and videos on it.
On my left I can see a big, big Panasonic TV
with noise bursting out of it.

Hearing my mum in the kitchen making a warm cup of cocoa
for me and my sister.
I can hear the familiar voice of my mum saying, 'Have a good time
at school then Tom!'

I smell the sweet scent of a burning candle.

Touch a soft, cuddly, friendly cat as it curls round your legs.

Taste the sweet soft drink as it makes its way
through your mouth.

Tom Tarrant (8)
Ubley Primary School

Home From School

Seeing Tammy my mad cat running around.
Seeing the TV.
Seeing the comfy sofa like I want to jump on it.
Seeing the cupboard and I want to dig in for food.

Hearing a miaow from my mad cat.
Hearing someone saying 'Feed the cat please.'
Hearing the boiling loudly.

Tasting a lovely drink.
Tasting some nice sticky sweets.
Tasting scrummy chocolate melting in my mouth.
Having a scrummy drink as soon as I get home.

Smelling my scrummy drink.
Smelling lush food.
Smelling a mad cat.

Lisa Barry (8)
Ubley Primary School

Home From School

Seeing Mum make a drink
Blackcurrant, my favourite.
Seeing a biscuit on the table,
Is that one for me?

Hearing my sister crying and whinging
Hearing the TV screaming.

Smelling a dog standing around me.
Smelling my sweet tea in the oven.

Touching clothes silky and smooth
Feeling my biscuit, crunchy, crumbly.

Yum biscuits going round my mouth, crunch, crunch,
Tasting the smell of the best tea in the world,
Burgers and chips.

Daniel Stuckey (9)
Ubley Primary School

Home From School

Home from school seeing a bounding dog leaping up,
Sniffing eagerly skidding around.
Seeing bones spread over the carpet,
Stables out with ponies in.
Big black sofa with huge red cushions.
Hundreds of black hairs lying messily on the floor.
Dog chasing tail trying to show off.

Tasting biscuits crumbling away and being eaten by the dog.
Tasting solid hard chocolate teeth eating up.

Smelling tea being cooked.
Smelling whiffs of horses from my riding clothes.
Smelling biscuits and juice wafting in the air.

Touching horses, moving them around.
Touching my dog's rough back and his soft fur.
Touching the keys at the piano as I make music.

Hearing the floor being scratched and skidded on.
Hearing soft music playing from another room.
Hearing the mooing of the cows in the distance.
Hearing the birds singing their tuneless song.

Harriet Walton (9)
Ubley Primary School

Home From School

Seeing a door waiting to be opened
Seeing a pool table, it is my turn
But I don't feel like it.
Going in to watch TV but I can't.
Seeing my brother and sister squabbling
Over the buttons.
Seeing my dad painting.

Hearing my brother crying because he can't get his own way.
Hearing the TV roaring, the laugh of my family echoing
Through my mind.

Smelling tea cooking
Smelling chocolate cake
Smelling the fragrance of the paint.

Touching the pool stick
Touching my biscuits crunching in my mouth
Touching eggs as I collect them.

Tasting tea as it swivels into my mouth
Tasting blackcurrants in my drink
Tasting my snack which is coated in chocolate.

Henry Chamberlain (8)
Ubley Primary School

Home From School

Seeing a warm furry cat running downstairs
Seeing the TV saying 'Come sit, watch.'
Seeing tea being made
What could it be?

Smelling the whiff of crunchy fried haddock.
Smelling sweet perfume
Drifting down the stairs.

Hearing Mum talking all about school,
TV loudly shouting on and on
Hearing the radio singing loudly.

Touching the soft warm fur of a cat
Touching the TV buttons
Touching the chocolate biscuits
Crumbling in my hands.

Tasting fresh poured orange juice
Tasting chocolate melting in my mouth
Biting into a nutritious orange.

Juliet Whittam (8)
Ubley Primary School

Home From School

Seeing a very excited puppy just about to wee
A very lazy, fat, fluffy cat resting on the arm of the settee
welcoming, staring at me.
Mum, arms out wide, ready to give me a welcoming hug.

Hearing the miaowing of a fat hungry cat waiting for his tea.
Opening a full biscuit tin and the pouring of refreshing squash
pattering in a glass cup.

Touching fluffy, warm fur of an exhausted cat resting on my bed,
Needle-sharp teeth of a playful puppy chewing,
tugging at my sleeve.

Tasting a crunchy, chocolate biscuit on the end
of my watering tongue.
Sugary sweet orange juice in my dry thirsty mouth.

Smelling delicious casseroles giving off a warm fishy whiff,
The meaty smell of processed dog and cat food
letting off a horrible pong.

Nancy Inman (8)
Ubley Primary School

Home From School

When I get home from school
I can see another door.
I walk in straight through the door
Walking into the living room.
Switching on the TV buttons.
When I walk out of the sitting room
Running up the stairs sniffing in the air
I find something big that I think has been
Sniffing down a rabbit hole.
When I come out of my bedroom I love to hold
And touch the banister.
Jumping down the stairs sliding off the banister.
When I walk into the kitchen
I can hear my mum cooking tea
With all the pots and pans clattering
Ding-dong, ding-dong.
After that I feel hungry and I can taste
All the biscuits waiting for me.

Harry Chubb (7)
Ubley Primary School

The Monster!

I saw a monster she said her name was Mary
Then she said she had a cousin called Berry.
She looked like she had three noses
One eye and four fingers on one hand
And on the other she had three fingers.
She had eighteen toes and her big fat bum shows.
The monster likes to play and after she says 'Boo'
It bumps out of the cupboard and always is covered.
My monster likes to climb up trees then she's scared of peas.
The monster wriggles around and around
After he falls flat on the ground.

Laura Withey (8)
Whitehall Primary School

My Monster's . . .

My monster's in my bed
My monster's in my bath
My monster's in clothes
My monster's in my hair.

This monster is terrifying
He smells like sweating socks
This monster's head is like a bed
He makes me have the chickenpox.

He takes by books
He takes my shoes
He is a cook
He takes my drinks.

He has a pig nose on his head
My monster has nails on his eyes
He has got pegs on his legs
He has a drink on his arm.

Olivia Thomas (8)
Whitehall Primary School

The Monster Poem

A monster lives in my house
He is so ugly
And has a friend called Suly
That's the monster who lives in my house.

The monster who lives in my house
He is red
And creeps up my bed
And bites off my head.

The monster who lives in my house
When he comes in
He has a great big fin
That's the monster who lives in my house.

Josh Barnett (9)
Whitehall Primary School

Monsters

Monsters can be scary,
Monsters can be solid,
Monsters can be wiggly,
Monsters can be horrid,
But my monster's nice!

My monster's as big as a mansion
He's thirty-nine feet tall
When he comes to visit me
He smashes through the wall
He's got a friend!

His friend is Mr Blobby
He gets me into trouble,
When I have a bath he makes me feel dry,
Coz he blows up all the bubbles.
This is how I feel.

Sometimes monsters make me unhappy
Sometimes they comfort me
But I know monsters can be fun
Especially after tea.
    They're not going to eat me!

Olivia Collins (9)
Whitehall Primary School

The Monster Of The Dead

The monster of the dead
He creeps through your house
And he slips through your door
As quiet as a mouse.

When you are very fast asleep
He breaks all your chairs
And even before you know it
He's eating your Dad's chest hairs.

He goes downstairs
He tries to eat your dog
And he goes outside
And floats through the fog.

He searches through the alley
Looking for a bin,
He tries to find a fish
And when he does, he starts eating its fin.

So he gets pretty bored
He goes to his grave
He goes down to the underworld
To have another shave.

Alan Gardner (8)
Whitehall Primary School

My Monster

My monster has a big head
My monster doesn't sleep in a bed
He has three noses
They all smell like roses.

He still smells like he just came out of the loo
He said, 'Look at my three noses
They all smell of roses!'

My monster has a big head
He should be dead, instead
He shouldn't be still alive
Because he smells like chives.

He smells like gone off malt
He also smells of salt
So this is how it ends
Me and my monster being friends.

Chelsea Owen (8)
Whitehall Primary School

Monster Disaster

I search around my room
To try and find my book
I saw something red
Then I saw it took.

It ate up all my dinner,
It looks like a pear
I saw it was a monster
So I hid behind my bear.

I feel very scared
Especially in bed
He's as big as a giant
But he is never being fed.

Chloe Nicholls (8)
Whitehall Primary School

The Monster In The House

It hides behind the cupboard
It lives in the garden
It scares you like a dragon
That makes you shout out loud.

He is red in the darkness
And green in the light.
He smells like rotten fish
And he is as fat as a dish.

He eats all your books
He has a hairy foot
He wears a black hat
He dislikes cats.

Brodi Osborne (9)
Whitehall Primary School

Monsters

Monsters in the bathroom
Monsters in the living room
Monsters in the kitchen
Monsters upstairs.

This monster is weird
This monster is flobby
This monster has a beard
This monster is watching Nobby.

Monsters in my loft
Monsters in my back garden
Monsters in my front garden
Monsters in my bedroom.

Stefanie Lamch (9)
Whitehall Primary School

The Thing

The thing gives me the shivers
It looks like a black bat black lizard
Its nose has boils and warts
Just like a bad wizard.
It just comes at dark,
But smells of eggs.
It comes just to my house
As quick and as silent as a mouse.
He or she goes to the hamster,
And lives in a dumpster.
I turn the light off to go to sleep
But then I hear a horrible cheep.
I turn the light back on and there is a shape,
My cat.
Phew.

Cristobal Arnaiz (8)
Whitehall Primary School

What Is The Moon?

The moon is a frozen waste, a smooth icy sea,
Like a golf ball resting on a jet-black tee.
The moon is a crystal ball, for a gypsy with second sight,
Like a diamond sparkling in the sun's clear light.
The moon is a giant's tooth, abandoned by the tooth fairy,
Like a snowball in a black gloved hand, all hairy.
The moon is a silver coin, dropped down Heaven's drain,
Sometimes like a crescent, until it becomes whole again.
The moon is like a football, silver-white and grey-black,
White like a swan's plumage, when it fluffs its feathers back.
It's as round as the Earth, facing it with pride,
The beautiful pearl of the sky.

James Braidley (10)
Winford CE Primary School

What Is Wind?

Wind is giant breath,
Beginner of storms,
Breakers of trees,
Cause of tidal waves,
Wind is giant breath.

Wind is the unseeable
Beginner of rain,
Breakers of homes,
Cause of earthquakes,
Wind is the unseeable.

Wind is the dead,
Beginner of lost hopes,
Breakers of lives,
Cause of nightmares,
Wind is the dead.

Wind is the howl of wolves,
Beginner of noise,
Breakers of darkness,
Cause of good thoughts,
Wind is the howl of wolves.

Wind is the bringer of light,
Beginner of blackness,
Breakers of depression,
Cause of imagination,
Wind is the bringer of light.

But does wind exist?
Can we see it?
We can hear it.
We can't smell it.
But does wind exist?

Thea House (10)
Winford CE Primary School